A GUIDE TO
PRACTICAL SPEECH TRAINING

A GUIDE TO
PRACTICAL
SPEECH TRAINING

By
GORDON LUCK
B.Sc., F.C.L.M., L.T.C.L.,
L.L.C.M.(T.D.), A.L.A.M.(Hons.)
Examiner, Adjudicator and Tutor in Speech and Drama

BARRIE & JENKINS
London Melbourne Sydney Auckland Johannesburg

Barrie & Jenkins Ltd

An imprint of the Hutchinson Publishing Group

17-21 Conway Street, London W1P 6JD

Hutchinson Group (Australia) Pty Ltd
30-32 Cremorne Street, Richmond South, Victoria 3121
PO Box 151, Broadway, New South Wales 2007

Hutchinson Group (NZ) Ltd
32-34 View Road, PO Box 40-086, Glenfield, Auckland 10

Hutchinson Group (SA) (Pty) Ltd
PO Box 337, Bergvlei 2012, South Africa

First published 1975
Reprinted in 1977, 1978 and 1982
© Gordon Luck 1975

Printed in Great Britain by The Anchor Press Ltd
and bound by Wm Brendon & Son Ltd
both of Tiptree, Essex

ISBN 0 214 20036 1

CONTENTS

FOREWORD

In 1958, the late Harry Johnson published his volume *Practical Speech Training*, which was subsequently adopted by the London College of Music as the theoretical basis for the examinations in Speech. In recent years however, some aspects of speech theory have undergone substantial modification and necessary changes have had to be made. As a result the present *Guide to Practical Speech Training* has been produced.

This book is intended to assist both students and teachers in general speech practice and preparation for examinations. In the earlier chapters, extensive alterations and supplements have been made to stimulate the reader's awareness and appreciation of sound and movement. The standard accounts of breathing and voice production are followed by a more detailed classification and description of all English speech sounds. In addition, numerous exercises are given both for articulation and all possible spellings of each sound.

To equip the reader for a practical comparative study of various speech phenomena, a chapter on speech faults has been introduced, outlining most of the commonly recurring errors or slovenly utterances, and remedial advice is given on their eradication. This, coupled with an enlarged section on developing vocal variety, aims to encourage the reader to explore the workings of the human voice in greater depth. The book concludes with some practical hints concerning speaking in public.

It must be noted, of course, that no book on speech training and oral communication can be an equivalent substitute for a good teacher. The *Guide to Practical Speech Training* should therefore serve as a supplement to genuine and competent effort in the teacher-pupil relationship, by providing the necessary technical information. I hope that the present volume meets this expectation, particularly for those whose interest in studying it is inspired by a sincere wish to enchance their speaking skill.

I should like to acknowledge the help given to me by Mrs Annette Garcia and Mr Hynek Cioch in the preparation of this volume.

GORDON LUCK
1974

CHAPTER ONE

SOUND EAR TRAINING

1 Dylan Thomas at the start of "Under Milkwood" gives the narrator this line: "To begin at the beginning". If one tries to apply that to speech training, it is very difficult to decide where the beginning lies. Is it, for example, technically starting with the breath, or the muscles controlling it, or the nerves controlling the muscles, or the mind controlling the nerves? What, however, stimulated the mind — a sight, or a sound — an emotion, or a recall from the past? Once the chain has been put into motion what other factors are brought into action to modify the beginning, the loudness, the quickness, the pauses, the subtle glides and use of colouring in speech, all contributing to the final effect?

From this very brief introduction you should appreciate that effective speaking is a very complex affair, requiring discrimination in the use of all aspects of vocal technique plus the ability to choose the best vocabulary, phrases and structures in order to make your speech coherent and logical. Superimpose on this the personality, dramatic and emotional factors and you have a challenge which is both demanding and exciting. The study of speech is a fascinating subject. Those who master it to some degree are not short of rewards. Those who conquer it will find abundant satisfaction in the use of our wonderful gift of voice.

2 It all starts at birth with a smack — a sound and sensation — followed by a cry. Our lungs have filled with air and we give vent to our feelings for having been delivered into the cold world where we shall have to speak in many ways, communicating, declaiming, cajoling, persuading, arguing, comforting, expounding, chatting, and philosophising, until the day we no longer have any breath left with which to utter. Coupled with this gift of speech is the gift of hearing. Those unfortunate people who are born deaf are also mute, until remedial action is taken. We learn to speak by imitation. We listen to

others and from them learn our sounds and expressions, both vocal and verbal.

In this opening chapter, we shall deal with sounds — both in general and in particular. The general aspects will refer to the effects of natural sounds and noises on the ear and how we can improve our appreciation of them. The sounds in particular will deal with an analysis of the sounds we use in speech.

SOUNDS AROUND US

3　There are sounds all around us all the time. Some are natural, some are man-made. It is a very good exercise to make a note of the sounds you hear at a particular moment or over a period of time. Or you could list the sounds associated with a particular place or with a certain activity. Once you have done this, decide whether they are pleasant to your ear or not. Next, if possible, try to imitate the sounds; some you will find very difficult to reproduce. Determine which of the sounds you can make with your voice help imitate the sounds you hear. Here are some examples:

Natural sounds	**Man-made sounds**
the sea churning on stones	*a train rattling*
the wind blowing	*a typewriter clattering*
the thunder crashing	*a hammer knocking*
the birds singing	*a bell ringing*
a wolf howling	*a siren wailing*
a cat purring	*a hooter sounding*
a dog barking	*a gun reporting*
an owl hooting	*a drill boring*

Now think of words that describe the sounds made by the following. Say the words aloud and listen to the effect they have on the ear. Are they effective, descriptive words? Can you imitate the actual sound involved? Here is the list:

Frogs, cows, sheep, lions, bees, mice, hens, donkeys, rain, a door knocker, a whip, cart wheels, an engine starting, brakes abruptly stopping a car.

Let us now think of other words which are descriptive because of their sounds, for instance the movement associated with certain objects. Say the words and try to "perform" the actions. For example, with snakes a good word would be "slithering" which creates the effect of a wriggling, slippery action. As you say the word you could use your whole body undulating across the floor, or you could use your arms as two snakes slithering across a surface. Listen – "two snakes slithering across a surface". What a lot of 'S' sounds! This repetition of a sound at the beginning of a word is called **alliteration** and can be used to create effects in the ear.

Consider horses, the descriptive words could be *prancing, clopping, thundering, trotting, cantering.* Say the words and perform the movements. Use either the whole body or just your fingers on a table. Which of the words sounds like the lightest movement, which is the heaviest and which is the most sweeping?

The last example for you is an aeroplane. "Move" the following words and listen: *sweep, soar, glide, zoom, dip, climb, vibrate, undulate.* You could link the words as a continuous exercise, even though the aeroplane would have a bumpy flight. Which words convey a smooth movement? Which are rough? Which are sudden?

Now try the following – choose your words associated with movement, say and perform the words and **listen to them:**

a river	*a fire*	*an archer*
a tree	*a spider*	*a violinist*
sweet peas	*rain*	*a cook*

In case you are having difficulties in finding words, here is a random list connected with the above. Select the appropriate words and act them.

curl, trickle, spread, shoot, bend, tinkle, flow, flicker, crawl, bound, drop, scrape, mix, aim, droop, vibrate, slop, entwine, release, pluck, ponder, thunder, pound, blossom, fall, spark, wither, hammer, weave, glide, drip, batter, spurt, foam, meander, sear, stretch, devour, scorch, score.

Try thinking why these words are so effective on the ear. Could it be the sounds of which they are composed? Think about the various sounds in words as you carry out the next series of exercises.

4 **Sounds and places.** List the sounds you might hear in the following situations. Determine which sounds you can imitate and which you can perform. How does the choice of sounds aid the descriptive qualities? Which sounds perform this creation? I'll start you off with *the factory:*

whirr	press	cut
clank	stretch	bore
bang	twine	screw
hammer	shudder	saw
hoot	churn	plane
clash	slide	grind

Can you hear that certain of those words create an abrupt, short, staccato action, other words suggest a prolonged action? Why is this? Explore the words to find out.

Now take each of those words again and add *-ing* to each. What change do you hear?

Here are some more situations for you to choose the descriptive words associated with them:

the kitchen, the laboratory, the gymnasium, the garage, the fun-fair, bonfire-night.

5 **Sounds and activities.** As before, list words associated with different activities, say the words, perform them and listen to them. I'll start you off with *cleaning:*

polishing, brushing, dabbing, splashing, scrubbing, smoothing, pressing, dusting, hoovering.

Now try these: *gardening, clay modelling, boxing, hunting, sailing.*

6 By now you will appreciate that many words imitate the sounds made by animals *coo, moo, baa,* objects *whizz, creak* and actions *crack, swish.* This very important side of speaking and hearing is called **onomatopoeia.** Sometimes it is called **imitative modulation.**

Listen to the creation of effects through the artistic and

sometimes inspired choice of words in the following lines. Say the lines aloud and make the most of the onomatopoeic words:

Alone and palely loitering.
Summer, summer, summer, the soundless footsteps on the grass.
Blow, winds, and crack your cheeks! rage! blow.
Rumble thy bellyful! Spit, fire! spout rain.
The swinging waves pealed on the shore.
I hear lake water lapping in low sounds by the shore.

Now fades the last long streak of snow,
Now burgeons every maze of quick
About the flowering squares, and thick
By ashen roots the violets blow.

Now rings the woodland loud and long,
The distance takes a lovelier hue,
And drowned in yonder living blue
The lark becomes a sightless song.

Open any book of good poetry and search for the descriptive words. Observe the alliteration and onomatopoeia. Notice also that many ends of lines rhyme, — there is an identical choice of vowel and consonant. In the above verses we have *snow* and *blow, quick* and *thick, long* and *song, hue* and *blue.* This rhyme is called **consonance**. It is pleasing to the ear and helps to create the poetic form. In prose also there is often much play on onomatopoeia, although there is no rhyme. Certain vowels may be repeated for effect in verse or in prose: "As the *old* man *rested* his weary *bones* on the *bed,* he *felt* his life *slowly ebb* away." This repetitive use of identical vowel sounds is called **assonance**. Onomatopoeia, alliteration, consonance and assonance are all artistic devices which are used to impress or please the ear.

SOUNDS IN SPEECH

7 Let us now turn to some technical matters concerning the sounds we use in our speech. We will consider their effects on the ear and how they are joined together to make connected speech.

As you read this book you recognise patterns on the page called letters. The alphabet is a list of letters arranged in order. These letters are only used for spelling and writing, we cannot speak with letters, we speak with sounds. There are, in fact, many more sounds we use in speaking than letters used to represent them in writing. More details concerning this will be found in chapters five, six and seven. When we speak we use vowel and consonant sounds.

A **vowel** in speech is a sound produced in the voice box and is emitted through a free opening of the mouth. It is not hindered in any way, although the actual vowel sound produced is determined by the position of the tongue and lips (see chapters six and seven).

A **consonant** is a sound formed when breath or voice is stopped or hindered in some way by the speech organs (see chapter five).

Examples of vowels are heard in the following words, the letters representing the sounds are in italics:

d*a*y pl*ea*se h*ea*d n*o*t c*oo*l b*a*t kn*o*w fl*y* fl*ow*er m*ou*nd

Examples of consonants are heard in the following words:

*d*ot *p*en *g*aze *h*ole *th*at*ch*

You can collect words containing as many different vowel and consonant sounds as possible, and see how the same sounds are represented by different spellings.

8 **Syllables.** A syllable is a word or part of a word formed by one effort of the voice. It can be a vowel alone, certain consonants alone, or a collection of vowels and consonants.

Put your hands on your chest and say these words: *I, my, oh, pa-per, mutt-on, de-liv-er, ex-am-in-a-tion, con-ster-na-tion*. Did you notice to say the first three words you had to make a little squeeze of your chest, this is called the **voice effort**. The next two words required two efforts of the voice, hence they contain two syllables, the second in *mutton* should only contain the 'n' sound. Count up the number of syllables in the remaining words and feel the effort of the voice on each.

Syllables are not separated from each other, they flow together as do words where they are connected with one idea. The grouping of words into ideas is called **phrasing**. Individual phrases should not be broken, but there should be pauses to separate the phrases. More will be said about pauses in chapter nine. Take this quotation from a well known nursery rhyme:

> *Little Jack Horner,*
> *Sat in the corner,*
> *Eating his Christmas pie.*

There we have eleven words, but only three phrases. The three ideas are *Jack Horner, in a corner,* and *eating his pie.* To speak that rhyme it would be necessary to join together the first three words containing five syllables, then the next four with again five syllables, and finally the last four words with six syllables. To write the phrases as they should be spoken would be like this: *little-jack-horner/sat-in-the-corner/eating-his-christmas-pie.*

9 Having established what vowel and consonant sounds are, and the meaning of syllables and phrases, we can proceed to a little more study of the value of sounds in syllables and phrases. We'll begin by taking words which you should say aloud with as much expression as possible, trying to create the effects on the vowels and consonants which are mentioned after each word. After you have explored the sound values of the vowels and consonants in each word, put the words into suitable sentences or if you are very diligent try to use them in a short poem. These words contain long vowels:

breeze — feel the little wind start on the *br* then let it flow gently on the vowel to stop on the *z* sound, possibly in some trees.

sleep — don't make a hiss on the *s*, start to drift off on the *l* and slowly float away on the vowel to end in dreamland on *p.*

dream — by lingering on the vowel and *m* the dream can be pleasantly sustained, any shortening makes it a nightmare.

sweep — start the action on *sw* and swing away on the vowel to complete the action on *p.*

free   — freedom starts on *fr* and you are at liberty as long as the vowel lasts.

deep   — the drop starts on *d* and the depth is as long as the vowel; the end of the journey is a little bump on *p*.

creep   — this is a tiring movement started on *cr* quietly progressing on the vowel to stop on *p*.

stream   — a quiet start gives way to freedom of movement here which is prolonged by the *m* sound.

calm   — by prolonging the vowel and the *m* a most pleasant stillness is created.

balmy   — the night scented air can be sensed again with play on the long vowel and *m*.

dark   — leave the light on *d* and feel yourself going deeper and deeper into the night on the vowel. Lightly touch the *k* to show the movement is complete.

past   — start going backwards in time on *p* and continue further and further as the vowel is made longer and longer. You arrive on *st*.

vast   — a firework start is made on *v* which expands on the vowel to the furthermost limits on *st*.

bore   — a "nasty" vowel. The speaking starts on *b* and goes on and on as long as the vowel lasts. One could of course start drilling on *b* and cut the hole on the vowel.

stalk   — a prowling word, feel the progression forward on the vowel and carefully place the foot down on the *k*.

forge   — another progressive word. Overcome resistance on *f* and penetrate on the vowel to meet more resistance at the end.

cool   — linger on the vowel and *l* to produce the peaceful mood.

soothe and *smooth* also· produce tranquility when the vowel is lengthened. Don't roughen the effect by emphasising the *th* sound.

dirty and *murky* sound nasty with a low pitched vowel and a curling of the lips.

whirl and *swirl* have movement in them if a curl is given through the voice on the vowel and a gradual settling created on the *l*.

Here are words with short vowels:

Short actions are emphasised by keeping the vowel short and

making the consonants sharp in such words as: *twist, rip, tip, snip, snick, pick, pelt, slap, snap, trap, bat, tug, shove, slump, tot, flog, pull, push* (The last two can be prolonged by lengthening the final consonant).

Explore the following words to see what effects you can create on the vowels — feel the movements in a straight line or in curves:

plain	*higher*	*oily*	*groan*
drape	*coil*	*slope*	*howl*
fly	*hoist*	*croak*	*growl*

Quite often the consonants play a more important part than the vowels. Consider these words:

meander — a lovely leisurely stroll emphasised by the *m* and *n*.

limp — a painful shift of weight here from the *m* to the *p*.

lingering — the *l*, *r* and *ng* produce the dwelling effect. There is also music here.

swell — the inflation starts on *sw* proceeds rapidly on the vowel to the extremes on *ll*.

mist — the emphasis here is on the *s* which creates the dampness.

slush — a lot of liquid here if you play on *s*, *l* and *sh*.

float — an airborne *f* sweeps along on the vowel to stop on *t*.

grisly — nasty grumpy start on *gr* gives way to a fighting unpleasant *z*.

whistle — the sounds here penetrate the air if you make a slight *h* after the *w* and hiss the *s* a little.

sizzle — can you create the sausages cooking in the fat by playing on the *s* and *z*?

contract — the collapse starts on the first syllable and finally ends with two gasps on the *ct*.

The number of syllables can also be emphasised to create effects for the ear.

Here are the double moving words, hear the change of weight from the first to the second syllable:

toddle (young and bright)	*hobble* (old and painful)
waddle (large and fat)	*jostle* (firm and rude)

swagger (bold and strong)   *stagger* (sharp and erratic)
totter (unbalanced and unsure)   *topple* (up and down)

Many action words have double syllables. Express these through the voice: *batter, rattle, dandle, tinkle, wrinkle, shrivel, grumble, bumble.*

10   There are endless possibilities in experimenting with sounds in words and phrases of our language. It is a joyful search into the origin and mysteries of human voice, revealing its vast potential as well as tracing its limitations. It also contributes greatly to attaining a purity of sound, its clear distinction and dynamism, which is the first victory towards meeting the challenge of good speech.

To sum up our objectives in this respect — **listen** to good speech sounds, **improve** your speech sounds and **create** with speech sounds.

CHAPTER TWO

BODY TRAINING

The previous chapter dealt with sounds and the importance of training the ear to appreciate them. Another very important skill to be acquired in speech training is to have the body under complete control — a body which is relaxed and poised, and yet alert to undergo whatever may be demanded as the will directs.

RELAXATION

11 What is the importance of relaxation? To answer that question let us see what happens to the body when the extreme opposite to relaxation takes place, that is tension. A tense body is a stiff body. A person with tension looks rigid. The legs begin to tremble. The muscles and veins in the neck stick out. Sometimes ugly blotches of red break out around the neck and on the face. The face becomes strained and the eyes stare or even bulge. The fists are clenched and the breathing is laboured. Shoulders become raised and fixed. The mouth dries up. The speech is impaired because the breath is gasped and uncontrolled. The diction will be hesitant and at times sounds become confused and mixed up. The tone is hard and strangled and there is a lack of range and expression. In addition to all this, one cannot think clearly when one is tense — one either goes blank or becomes an ineffectual, faltering, mechanical body uttering restricted, jumbled uninteresting sounds.

What a lot of terrible things can happen with extreme tension. In fact, one can actually collapse. Tension is the chief enemy to good speech, so let us now see how relaxation can be acquired.

Achieving Relaxed State

12 First of all approach your speech work from the point of view of the mind. If you have to perform or speak in public, or even go

for an interview, there is an element of dread over the "ordeal".
What is there to be frightened of?

(a)   You may appear a fool.
(b)   You may forget your lines, your content, or your
       qualifications for a job.
(c)   The audience may be hostile.

Why should you feel a fool? As soon as you start to perform, speak
or talk, the first impression the audience receives is the visual one. If
you are tense and ill at ease, and avoid the idea of sharing an
experience with your hearers, you will feel that you are making an
idiot of yourself. You will, too, if your delivery is hesitant and
inarticulate. This idea of foolishness is further built up when you
imagine what the audience is thinking of you all the time.

To overcome point (a) carry out the bodily relaxation exercises
given later in this chapter, they will help you to stand correctly and
easily and to aid you in your movement and gesture including the
vital use of the face. Practise the articulation exercises given in
chapter five to ensure neat and accurate diction. Knowing your
speech is clear and correct is another hurdle crossed towards smooth
relaxed delivery. If you devote too much time to thinking of your
audience, you are not concentrating enough on your content and
presentation. Put your energy, especially at the start, into projecting
the substance of your poem, scene or talk. In public speaking, in
conversation or in the interview situation try to make eye contact
with as many of the audience as possible and use the face sincerely.
If a smile is in order let it arise from the heart and not merely from
the cheek muscles.

Inevitably point (b) is closely connected with (a). One tends to
forget if one is not thoroughly prepared. A scene, poem or a piece of
prose has to be studied to assimilate the thoughts contained therein.
This entails exploration into the ideas of the author. It includes
experimentation in the mode of presentation both vocally and
visually. There has to be background reading to understand how and
why the piece being performed was written. The more background
knowledge you can obtain concerning the writing, the more
proficient, assured and convincing its public presentation will be.

With public speaking, again the idea of preparation is very
important. Research, study and more research must be made into all
aspects of your topic. This work may not manifest itself in the

actual number of points covered in the talk. Indeed one should choose the number of facets of the speech very carefully because a crowded speech can become a garbled mess leading to loss of memory, lack of fluency and induces tension. The background research gives you the confidence that you know your subject well and can answer any questions put by the audience at the end. More details concerning public speaking are given in chapter ten.

Point (c) rarely occurs, except for political addresses or debates. The former can be vitriolic and even violent, but I doubt whether the readers of this book will encounter these problems. Debates usually are conducted in an orderly fashion and often contain a lot of wit and humour. Again in these situations, well prepared work will help you to speak effectively.

Think of your audience as being on your side, as being friendly and sympathetic. You have been asked to speak or perform in public, therefore the audience wants to hear from you. Think of your performances as being a compliment from the audience to you.

Let us now consider supine exercises which are designed to free the body and mind from tension.

EXERCISES I. (THE BODY)

Be a Star
Lie down on your back and spread your arms, palms up to the side and open your legs. Stretch the limbs all together. Feel you are making a four-pointed star. Suddenly the star collapses. Feel the tension disappear.

Be a Hercules
In the same position, imagine that the body is being pushed down by a very heavy weight so that all parts of the body are being pressed into the ground. Suddenly the weight is removed. Feel yourself float off the ground.

Shake off Those Ants
In the same position, imagine you are tied to the ground, but you can wriggle. A colony of ants finds you and begin to crawl all over you. Commence to wriggle the body until the last ant leaves you. Then collapse.

Hot – Warm – Cold

Lie on your back, feet together, arms by your sides, hands lightly curled, fingers pointing towards the body. Close the eyes. Follow this sequence of feeling and seeing. Hot – red, gradually change to warm – yellow, then cool – green and finally freezing – ice blue. Reverse the sequence until you feel in a cosy red glow.

The Expanding Room

Slowly get up from the lying position, pausing to sit up, and then stand. Slowly stretch the whole body upwards raising the heels and arms. Think that you are going to touch the ceiling of a low room, this you do easily. Now that ceiling is going to be raised, as it happens you have to stretch more and more until you snap and crumple completely. Stand with the feet apart and try to push the walls of the room away from you. Decide it's too much work and flop.

Be a Rubber Puppet

Imagine you are made of rubber and there are strings attached to your shoulders which someone can pull from above. You are being pulled up and you find your limbs fly out in all directions. Even your feet are pulled off the ground at times. Finally the strings are cut and you flop to the ground. Stay there in a completely relaxed state for a few moments and appreciate how you feel when you are relaxed. Shake all parts of the body, then suddenly become rigid. After a moment or so flop completely.

Be Smoke in a Chimney

Stand comfortably and start to undulate the whole body starting at the feet (allow the heels to be raised from the floor). Imagine ripples moving up your body and flowing out of the top of your head. These ripples you are making move forwards and backwards. Now change and undulate from side to side. Imagine you are some smoke meandering up a chimney.

Be a Spinning Jenny

Start with each foot in turn and rotate from the ankles. Then start rotating all parts of the body, the knees, hips, shoulders, hands and the head (but gently). In the end all parts of the body should be making circular movements at the same time. Suddenly freeze the motion and then slowly melt until you are completely relaxed.

Be in a Waxwork's Fire
Pretend that you are some famous figure in history and you are in the waxworks. There is a fire. Feel yourself melting from the extremities, right to the core of your body.

Exercise each part of the body as follows:

1. Imagine playing the five finger exercise with your toes. Grip a pencil with your toes and write your name on the floor.
2. Perform a full knees bend.
3. Swing the hips from side to side.
4. Rotate the hips as if you were spinning a hoop around the waist.
5. Bend the trunk from the waist forwards and backwards, and side to side.
6. Shrug the shoulders up and down.
7. Rotate each shoulder separately and then together in opposite directions.
8. Circle the arms in a clockwise, then anti-clockwise direction.
9. Hold the arms out in front of you, fingers together. Try separating each finger in turn.
10. Perform five finger exercises in a rippling motion.
11. Stretch the neck, then contract it.
12. Bend the head from side to side, drop it forwards and backwards, turn it left and right, finally slowly circle the head stretching all the neck muscles in turn.

Exercise each part of the face as follows:

1. Try to move the scalp forwards and backwards.
2. Raise the eyebrows together, then one at a time.
3. Wink each eye in turn, then blink rapidly.
4. Screw the eyes up tightly, then open them as widely as you can.
5. Try to wiggle your ears.
6. Pull the nose from side to side using the cheek muscles.
7. Wrinkle the nose as if smelling something awful.
8. Put the lips into a smile, a pout, a snarl, and a leer.
9. Place the jaw forwards as for arrogance, and backwards as for stupidity.

10. Use the whole face to express such moods and emotions as happiness, dejection, anticipation, fear, disgust, horror, ridicule, innocence, anger, cunning, on the verge of tears, extreme exhaustion.

NB: **Do all the above exercises in series of three or four and develop a routine of practising different series on different occasions.**

You may have noticed that all these exercises designed to help you to relax are based upon sudden changes from tension or vigorous activity to an inert, relaxed state. That is the principle of relaxing. Other animals relax in this way — you must have seen a cat or a dog stretch itself before relaxing and then going to sleep.

EXERCISES II. (THE MIND)

13 These are motivated exercises and would be useful at the start of drama classes. They are graded for different age ranges, starting with young children.

Animal Capers
Pretend you are various animals and imitate the way they move around. For instance the wriggling of a snake, the hopping of a kangaroo, the fluttering of a bird, the leap of a lion, the spring of a cat, and so on. After some moments of movement let all the animals go to sleep.

Be a Leaf in a Storm
Imagine you are a leaf, stuck fast on a tree. You can hold on to a piece of furniture to represent the tree. Suddenly a wind starts blowing and rustles all the leaves at first only a little and then more and more until finally each leaf is torn from the tree and is swirled about. Finally the wind ceases and you flutter down to earth and lie still.

Be a Wicked Wolf
Imagine you are the wolf in the story of the three little pigs. Swell yourself and blow down all the houses except the one made of bricks.

Be a Clock-work Soldier
You are a clockwork soldier or doll. Feel yourself being wound up and then start to move very stiffly and slowly at first. After a few movements something goes wrong with the mechanism and you begin to move faster and faster until finally you fall to pieces.

A School of Mime
A group of mime is often very useful as an exercise in freeing the body and stimulating the imagination. Let a group of boys pretend they are putting up a tent. There are all sorts of occupational movements involving tension and relaxation, for instance, unpacking the heavy equipment, stretching out the tent, forcing in the poles and pegs, pulling ropes taut and so on. A group of girls could try their hand at miming spring cleaning. Here we have lifting, pushing, pulling, spreading, rubbing, wringing, and many more activities.

A Magic Balloon
Find a magic balloon and start to blow it up squeezing all your breath into it. Feel the balloon get larger and larger. Tie the end with string. Now this is a magic balloon and it is so big that it begins to lift you off the ground. Up you go and start to float around. Suddenly the balloon bursts and down you fall.

Alice in Wonderland
A good exercise for contracting the body is this one. Imagine you enter a square room. The door through which you have just entered locks behind you. In the opposite wall there is another door, but smaller than the first one. It is unlocked and you go through it into a smaller room. Again the door locks behind you, but once more there is a door facing you but it is smaller than the previous two, nevertheless you manage to get through it into yet another room which is much smaller than the other three. This is repeated and the room is smaller and you are all screwed up. There is just one door to go through; very slowly you manage to get each part through it to find eventually you have escaped into the open. Feel the expansion of the body.

Be a Bare-foot Runner
Think you are running along without shoes and socks. First you cross a firm lawn which is very warm in the sun, next you come to

some jagged stones (emphasise the leaping here), a belt of very, very hot sand follows and finally this gives way to a swamp of quicksand. Feel yourself being dragged down.

Be a Lumberjack
Pretend you are lumberjacks. Work with a partner to saw down a tree using a two handled saw. Use axes as well and feel the sudden resistance as the blade hits the wood.

Tug-o-War
Form half of an imaginary tug-o-war team. Heave away against your make-believe opponents.

A Caveman's Trip
Emerge from a cave onto a very narrow ledge beyond which is a sheer drop to rocks below. Opposite you is another ledge about three feet away. A sturdy piece of tree is growing out of the rock above the ledge. Decide to cross the chasm — aim for the tree — stride across and hold on desperately. Recover your nerve and edge your way inch by inch along the ledge to safety. Feel the relief.

Peep and Duck
Creep up to a high wall. Place your finger tips on the top and stretch yourself up on your toes to peep over. Look to right and left. Suddenly you are spotted and you duck down out of sight.

Be a Charlady
You are in a narrow corridor which has high shelves on either side running along its length. On the right shelf is a large vase. Decide to lift the vase down for cleaning. Feel its weight. Relax as you dust it, then stretch up and replace it on the left shelf.

Be a Tomato Plant
Start as a plant seed which is very compact. Swell as you germinate and begin to sprout upwards. Shoot towards the sky and spread out your stalks. Let the branches become heavy with fruit. Finally at the end of the season droop, wither and die.

Note: Although on the surface these exercises do not seem to have direct connection with speech training, a little reflection after you have tried some of them, will reveal to you that they are designed to promote relaxation both in the body and mind; also flexibility of all muscles, and a stimulation of the imagination. Once this is achieved and the imagination is triggered off, you are in a position to interpret your spoken work in an artistic way.

POSTURE

14 To conclude this chapter let us consider the posture which should be adopted for speech work which doesn't require characterisation. Posture is the position and carriage of the body. Obviously a specific character will demand its own particular posture. However, on the whole, try to observe the points given below.

Feet. Slightly apart. The weight of the body resting mainly upon one foot; the other foot rests lightly upon the ground to form a means of balance and support. The weight should be shifted and the balance-foot changed quite often while standing. This should occur without conscious effort and quite unobserved by the audience. Shuffling and swaying should be avoided, also any stiffening or "freezing" of the position.

Legs. The leg of the foot bearing the weight of the body should be braced but not stiffly locked. The leg of the balance-foot should be quite relaxed.

Waist. There should be a slightly tight or "belted" feeling around the waist; the abdominal muscles should be slightly indrawn.

Body. Erect, with no feeling of stiffness around the chest.

Shoulders. Square, but avoid any rigid, soldier-like attitude.

Chin. Level; neither tilted upwards, poked forward, or depressed. This prevents the neck and throat muscles from becoming tight — a most important necessity for good speech and voice production.

Eyes. A sincere focus should be adopted, never use a fixed stare or the opposite — restless darting of the eyes. See the scenes you are describing in recital work. For dramatic work, obviously, you use the eyes to observe the situation and other characters. When speaking in public, make eye contact with your audience. Finally, when you say a poem such as a lyric or ode, don't stare directly into the eyes of your audience, when you reflect, look over and beyond your listeners.

Head. Steady, with good front face direction. Avoid nodding or shaking the head when speaking.

Arms. Hanging quite loosely by the sides — nearly touching the sides, never held out and away from the body, and not pressing or hugging the sides.

Hands. Quite relaxed from the wrists. The fingers should be slightly curled, with the thumbs to be seen; the thumb to be lightly touching the curled forefinger.

Do not think about how you stand when speaking or reciting, or you will become posture-conscious, and you will begin to feel perched or poised in one position. Then you may become embarrassed or nervous. Stand comfortably and then forget all about it during the whole time you are speaking or reciting.

CHAPTER THREE

BREATHING

15 Once the body has become relaxed, you are well on the way to presenting yourself successfully for speech work in public. The next step is to develop what may be called the motive power of speech, namely the breath. Breath is the **excitor** in speaking, it starts the whole process off. It is obvious then, that it is very important that our breathing method must be secure i.e. the right amounts of air can be taken in and let out easily in a controlled manner. This chapter will therefore deal with the physiology of breathing and the organs used, the mechanics of the process and exercises for its improvement and control.

PHYSIOLOGY OF BREATHING

16 As we breathe in, we notice that our chests enlarge. You can measure the extent of this expansion by placing your hands flat on the lower part of the chest before breathing in, so that the finger tips meet at the breast bone. As you breathe in the fingers are not only pushed outwards and upwards, but apart as well. The reverse happens on breathing out, the fingers fall back to their original position. This whole cycle of breathing in and out is called **respiration**. As has been said, respiration is in two phases — breathing in, which is called **inhalation** or **inspiration**, and breathing out, **exhalation** or **expiration**. During inhalation the chest is expanded, its volume increases. During exhalation the reverse takes place. Another name for the chest is the **thorax** which forms the upper part of the torso. The thorax contains the lungs and the heart. The thorax is a bony, cage-like structure consisting of the spinal column, running down the back, the **sternum** or breast bone, running down the front, the ribs, the shoulder blades and the collar bones.

Try this exploration of the thorax: place your finger tips on your shoulders at the front. At the top of the shoulders just before you come to the neck you will feel a bone which goes from the shoulder on each side to the centre of the body at the bottom of the neck. These two bones are the collar bones. If you let your hands travel downwards along the centre of the chest, you trace a short bone called the sternum. Now let your hands spread out from the sternum on either side, the bones you feel are the ribs. Try counting how many pairs of ribs you have.

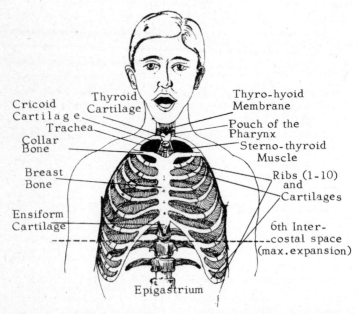

Fig. 1 Front view of chest with ribs exposed, showing where movement of diaphragm is felt (Epigastrium) when ribs are expanded.

Do you notice that at the end of the sternum the ribs curve away more and sweep downwards? Where do they end? At the back? Yes, the first ten pairs of ribs do go around the body and join the spine. Lastly, try to feel your back bone, or spine.

THORAX

Figure 1 shows you the main features of the thorax. There are twelve pairs of ribs. The first five pairs are connected directly to the sternum at the front and to the spine at the back. The next five pairs are connected by cartilage indirectly to the sternum, but are joined directly to the spine. There are two more pairs of ribs which are much smaller than the rest, these are only attached to the spine and are called the floating ribs. If you feel along the base of the thorax at the back you can locate these floating ribs. The arrangement of the ribs is such that they can swing outwards and upwards.

A good demonstration of this swing is seen if you place your finger tips together about fifteen inches from the body in front of your chin, let the elbows drop. Gradually raise the elbows without moving the hands. The distance between the elbows increases in roughly the same way as the chest is expanded when the ribs are raised. Besides there being an expansion of the chest from side to side, there is also a front to back expansion. Feel this as you take a deep breath by placing the palm of one hand across the body near the end of the sternum while the palm of your other hand is held on the back part of the ribs.

17 The **lungs** are protected by the thorax. There are two lungs, a left and a right, each divided into lobes, two on the left and three on the right. Figure 2 gives details of the shape and features of the lungs. As you see, each lung is almost semi-circular. The lungs consist of a spongy tissue made up of a countless number of air tubes and air sacs or **alveoli**. Intermingling with these air sacs are millions of tiny blood vessels. It is here that the exchange of carbon dioxide for oxygen takes place, and oxygen enters the blood to be circulated around the body to keep us alive. The air sacs and lungs themselves are inert bodies, that is, they do not have the power to perform any muscular activity and hence are not by themselves capable of taking in air. The lungs merely store the air, they cannot suck it in, any more than a paper bag can do it. The air must therefore be forced into the lungs.

18 Air enters and leaves the lungs via the air passages. Let us trace the outgoing passage. From the air sacs the air passes into air

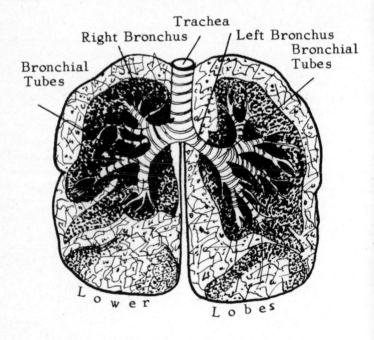

Fig. 2 The Lungs showing bronchial tree with branches.

tubes which join to form the **bronchioles** which are tributaries carrying air to the two **bronchi** (singular = bronchus). The bronchus from each lung join to form the wind pipe or **trachea**. Air passes up the trachea through the voice box or **larynx** into the back of the mouth or **pharynx**. From there it passes out through the mouth, or if the soft palate is lowered, through the nose.

19 Now we turn to the mechanism of breathing. As mentioned earlier, the lungs cannot take in air by themselves, it has to be forced in. "Nature abhors a vacuum". If the handles of a pair of bellows are

pulled apart, air is forced into the bag of the bellows by the outside air pressure. The same principle operates with a dropper. As the rubber bulb is squeezed, some air is expelled from the tube. When the end of the tube is placed in a liquid, the outside air pressure on the surface of the liquid forces the liquid into the tube as the bulb ceases to be squeezed. Think of the thorax as a pair of bellows; if the size of the thorax is increased, then a vacuum would be formed in the lungs. The outside air pressure forces air into the lungs to prevent that vacuum from being created.

The next question to answer is how is the thorax enlarged and what particular muscles are involved in the breathing process.

MUSCLES FOR BREATHING

20 There are many muscles used to control inhalation and exhalation. The first three sets described below are the most important, but mention will be made of others which also help.

The intercostal muscles. These muscles move the ribs. The first thing to remember is that muscles act by contraction — they pull, they cannot push. The intercostal muscles lie between adjacent ribs and by contraction they lift the ribs. In breathing in, we want the ribs to move outwards and upwards and for exhalation the ribs must be brought back to their original position. As muscles cannot push — they can only pull — it follows that we must have two sets of intercostal muscles: one set to pull the ribs out and a second set to pull them back again. The first set is called the **outer** or **external intercostal muscles** and lie obliquely between each pair of ribs running in a direction upwards and away from the sternum. As these muscles contract, the ribs are pulled outwards and upwards, thus widening the thorax. This is the action during inhalation. When exhaling there are two possibilities. The weight of the ribs and the elasticity of the lungs may cause the thorax to collapse, thus expelling air from the lungs. With the more controlled breathing for speech, the second set of intercostal muscles is brought into play. These are the **inner** or **internal intercostal muscles.** These too lie obliquely between the ribs but in the opposite direction to the external intercostal muscles, that is sloping down away from sternum. When these muscles contract, they pull the ribs downwards and inwards thus forcing air out of the lungs.

The two sets of intercostal muscles act in opposition. This is called the **antagonistic action** of muscles. In fact, most muscles of the body are paired, one set pulls a bone in one direction and another set reverses the movement, e.g. one set of muscles pulls the forearm upwards, another set straightens the arm again. So it is with the intercostal muscles – the outer set helps inhalation, the inner set is used for exhalation.

Central Tendon

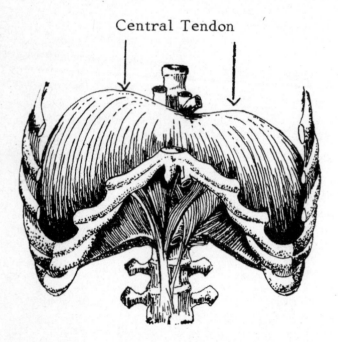

Fig. 3 The Diaphragm

The diaphragm. This muscle is very important for inhalation. It forms the floor of the thorax and the roof of the abdomen [see figure 3]. The diaphragm is double dome-shaped with the right dome a little higher than the left. At the centre is what is called the central tendon, and from this tendon the fibrils (small parts of muscles) extend to the lower ribs, the sternum and the spine. The effect is very roughly like an open umbrella. When the muscular fibres contract, the central tendon is pulled down. This downward action increases the vertical dimension of the thorax and thus provides extra space for the lungs to be filled with air.

We said earlier that muscles act in pairs. Here we have the body's largest muscle which has just contracted during inhalation. To exhale the diaphragm must rise again. For this another set of muscles is required.

The abdominal muscles. These muscles form the wall of the abdomen. You can see them work if you "pull in on your tummy". There are four sets of abdominal muscles: two pairs running obliquely, one running up the front of the abdomen and the fourth set, **the transverse abdominal muscles,** run around the body like a girdle or cummerbund. When the diaphragm descends during inhalation, the abdominal contents are pushed somewhat and cause the upper abdominal wall, which is relaxed slightly, to move forward a little. Now comes the antagonistic action. When we wish to exhale, particularly for speech purposes, the abdominal muscles contract and pull in the abdominal wall.

When this happens the abdominal contents are squeezed slightly and push up on the lower side of the diaphragm. With increasing contraction of the abdominal muscles and gradual relaxation of the fibres of the diaphragm, the diaphragm rises under control.

This action can be illustrated with a balloon on a table. Put your hands flat on top of the inflated balloon; these represent the diaphragm. Ask a friend to place his hands around the balloon; these represent the transverse abdominal muscles. The balloon represents the abdominal contents. As you press your hands downwards (descent of the diaphragm), the balloon bulges and the friend's hand must give way to this (relaxation of the abdominal muscles). This is illustrating inhalation. For exhalation, the friend applies pressure to the sides of the balloon which is thus squeezed upwards against your hands, which rise as the diaphragm does during exhalation.

BREATHING FOR SPEECH

21 This method is called **intercostal diaphragmatic breathing** and is the best method of breathing for speech. Let us summarise the main points:

1. **inhalation**   external intercostal muscles contract,
                         internal intercostal muscles relax,
                         ribs drawn upwards and outwards,
                         diaphragm descends,
                         abdominal muscles relax.

2. **exhalation**   abdominal muscles contract,
                         diaphragm rises,
                         { external intercostal muscles relax,
                           internal intercostal muscles contract,
                           ribs drawn downwards and inwards.

Thus in breathing there are two cycles — the movement of the thorax and the diaphragmatic action. The two actions are not, in fact, quite simultaneous, the rib movement occurring slightly before the diaphragmatic movement during inhalation, with the reverse happening when breathing out.

22 When control is demanded during exhalation whilst speaking, a slight modification to the intercostal diaphragmatic method of breathing is made. As has just been mentioned, there are two distinct movements made during breathing — the **rib movement** and the **diaphragmatic movement**. It is possible to adopt the following method of breathing which relies on the separation of these two movements. The thorax is expanded and the diaphragm lowered as for the usual inhalation. Next, the abdominal muscles contract indirectly controlling the rise of the diaphragm. Now comes the modification.

Instead of the ribs returning to their original position, they are held out by the prolonged contraction of the external intercostal muscles. A replenishment of air then takes place as the diaphragm lowers to be followed, in turn, by further contraction of the abdominal muscles during exhalation. Thus we have a kind of pumping action by the diaphragm as the thorax is kept expanded.

If a very long phrase is to be spoken and the abdominal muscles cannot contract any more, then the internal intercostal muscles can be brought into action. They contract and cause more air to be forced from the lungs to produce speech. This method of breathing is called **rib reserve breathing**.

23 There are many advantages in using the intercostal diaphragmatic method of breathing for speech, and this also includes rib reserve breathing.

(a) the lungs are speedily replenished with sufficient air.
(b) there is good control over the diaphragm by the abdominal muscles, thus ensuring an even flow of exhaled air.
(c) the method avoids gasping for air at the end of long phrases.
(d) there is adequate projection and the fault of dropping the voice at the ends of phrases is avoided.
(e) no strain is placed on the larynx.

24 There are other muscles involved in the breathing process, in fact there are dozens of sets, but unless one is a student of anatomy, a study of them here would serve little purpose. However, more advanced students of speech should note the following:

The pectorals. One set of these muscles extends from the collar bone and sternum to the upper five or six ribs. Another set extends from the shoulder blade to the third, fourth and fifth ribs. Their action is to pull these ribs upwards. The pectoral muscles act on the front of the thorax.

The levatores costarum work on the ribs at the back of the body. They extend from each bone in the spine to the point where the first and second ribs join the spine. So, on contraction, these muscles lift all the ribs at the back.

OTHER METHODS OF BREATHING

25 Having discussed the correct method of breathing for speech let us investigate other possible methods of breathing. When we are not speaking, or when resting or even when asleep, our breathing could be described as **tidal breathing** or the **breathing of repose** or even **tranquil breathing**. We started to breathe this way from the day we were born and will do so as long as we live. This method of breathing is sufficient to keep all our essential functions going, such as the heart beat, blood circulation, etc. It is rhythmical and does not call into play the controlled movements of the muscles described

earlier. It is an entirely subconscious method of breathing, during which the diaphragm sinks very slightly and the lower ribs move outwards a little by the action of the external intercostal muscles. At the end of inhalation, the air is expelled by the recoil action of the lung tissue and the falling of the ribs by their own weight.

There is no action by the internal intercostal muscles. This method of breathing cannot sustain the voice when speaking with any force and certainly cannot be used for recital purposes.

26 **Abdominal breathing** is an incorrect method. This occurs when the diaphragm sinks too low (approximately three and a half inches compared with one and a half for intercostal diaphragmatic breathing). Consequently the abdominal contents are pushed down with considerable force and the abdominal wall protrudes in an unsightly fashion. The ribs are not used very much for lateral expansion of the thorax. On exhalation the abdominal muscles do not have enough control over the uprising diaphragm, which springs back, thus letting the breath out in one forceful gust. The outrush of air does not vibrate the vocal cords properly, and the sound escapes in a breathy rush which cannot be well sustained. There is often a noisy gap at each succeeding inhalation. The internal intercostal muscles are insufficiently geared into action in this method, because of incomplete expansion of the thorax.

27 **Clavicular breathing** is another method not to be recommended. The term "clavicular" is associated with the collar bones or clavicles. In this method, the shoulders are drawn upwards, as is the sternum and ribs. Consequently the diaphragm is literally squeezed out of action, because the thorax tends to become narrow and elongated. As only the narrow, upper part of the thorax is used for expansion, there is little air intake into the lungs. The breathing is shallow and uncontrolled, the tone is strained and it seems as if the speaker is out of breath. Clavicular breathing also results in facial strain, and general tension. Its continual use can be harmful. This method of breathing should therefore be avoided even when enacting dramatic situations; an emotional person does not heave with the shoulders, he works from the diaphragm.

BREATHING FAULTS

28 Apart from the incorrect methods of breathing, there are some breathing faults.

(a) Insufficient air may be inhaled thus resulting in gasping at the end of phrases followed by **noisy inhalation**. To avoid this try to phrase your sentences' sensibly and practise the breathing exercises given later to increase the capacity of the lungs in order to cope with any particularly long phrases.

(b) The tone may fade at the end of sentences, this is often called **dropping of the voice**. Avoid this by maintaining the pressure of the abdominal muscles during exhalation.

(c) A **tremolo** may be heard. This is a wobbling in the tone and is caused by lack of smooth contraction of the abdominal muscles during exhalation. The exercises given later will help here.

(d) A **rebound** occurs when the vocalised breath-flow continues after the final sound in a phrase. We get *it is good-uh – are you going-uh? – It's too far-uh.* Care must be taken to stop the vocalisation and the breath-flow towards the end of the final sound in the phrase.

(e) A slow control by the abdominal muscles is essential to avoid **breathy tone,** when too much breath is expelled with aspirate consonants. The effect is a sort of gale preceding vowels e.g. *t-hhh-ake a p-hhh-air of k-hhh-ipp-hhh-ers-hhh.* This surely must be a waste of breath economy.

BREATHING EXERCISES

29 At this stage it would be appropriate to concentrate on some breathing exercises to help capacity, rate of exhalation and inhalation, and projection. Always adopt an easy posture as described in chapter two, relax and concentrate on the movements of the thorax, diaphragm and abdominal muscles.

Abdominal wall
Feel the movements of the ribs and abdominal wall as you breathe in and out deeply. Place your hands on the area where the sternum

ends and the ribs curve away — the **epigastrium** as it's termed — feel
the to-and-fro action, which should be smooth and rhythmical.
Repeat this by placing the hands at the side and then at the back of
the rib cage. Feel that outward swing and also the backward thrust.
Place the hands, finger tips touching across the epigastrium, feel the
slight push forward on inhalation. Now quickly force the air out of
the lungs. Do you feel the pull in of the abdominal wall?

Timing of Silent Breath
Breathe in through the nose to a count of three raising the arms to
shoulder height. Gently and silently let the air out through the
mouth to a count of three. Repeat this exercise varying the number
of counts for the inhalation and exhalation, for instance, in 4 - out
4, in 2 - out 6, in 5 - out 5, in 2 - out 8 and so on. The timing of the
counting should be one per second. Repeat this exercise but
introduce a hold between breathing in and counting out. The hold
should be controlled by the cessation of muscular activity of the
thorax and abdomen, and not as the result of closing the throat.

Timing of Vocalised Breath
Try a similar exercise, but count the numbers on exhalation aloud.
Never force the final numbers just to see how far you can count in
one breath.

The Rib Swing
Try separately the two breathing actions, that is inhale and exhale,
using only the rib swing, then repeat concentrating on the diaphragm
and abdominal muscles. Finally take a deep breath through the nose
using all muscles, hold the breath for a moment and then pant out
using the pressure of the abdominal muscles.

Controlled Breath-flow
Take a straw and a glass of water. Inhale and blow through the straw
into the water. First try to make the flow of bubbles into the water
as regular as possible. Repeat this exercise three times. After a brief
rest try the exercise again, but this time let the bubbles emerge very
slowly at first and then gradually increase the rate. This is a very
good exercise for control of the breath flow.

Controlled Breath-force
Hold a sheet of flimsy paper with both hands about eight inches from your mouth. Hold it by the top corners so that the paper hangs down freely. Now blow gently towards the bottom of the sheet to make it swing away from you. Try to control the rate and force of exhalation to keep the paper at a constant angle. Repeat this experiment at different distances from your mouth.

Snatched Breath
Inhale through the mouth, start counting aloud directing the breath towards the opposite wall. After each three counts replace the breath quickly through the mouth. This method is called snatched breath technique.

Emotional Breath
As said earlier, the emotions stem from the diaphragm, under the control of the mind. Try these exercises which link breathing and emotion. Breathe in and feel what is happening to the diaphragm as you say *Oh!* expressing the following emotions. Use one breath for each exercise.

Emotions: calm, exasperation, anger, ridicule, dawning realisation, fatigue, irritation, disappointment.

You can make up many more exercises like this one. Try building up a scale of emotions and say a phrase on each. For instance take *I can't help it* and start by saying it as if you are exhausted, almost on the point of fainting. Then say it in a tired, weary voice. Next in disappointment. Work up to indifference, anticipation, excitement, and so on to extreme anger.

Whispering
Try stage whispering, working on the abdominal muscles. Any sentences given for practice in chapters, five, six and seven will serve the purpose.

FINAL NOTES ON BREATHING

30 Develop a habit of practising correct breathing daily; preferably where there is plenty of fresh air. Breathe in through the

nose, when not speaking. By doing this the air is warmed, moistened and filtered and hence the lungs are protected from chill and dirt. The warming occurs because the air has a longer journey to reach the lungs via the nasal passages rather than straight through the mouth into the throat. In the nose there are fine hairs which help to filter out dirt. There are also glands in the nose which secrete moisture. Of course, when you are speaking, mouth breathing is to be recommended as it is quicker and avoids any tendency to sniff through the nose. It also prevents any strained expression and avoids nasality when the soft palate is lowered as breath is taken through the nose.

Finally let your breathing for speech become second nature. Don't think about your breathing too much or you will become breath-conscious, and your thoughts will be devoted to the breathing activity and control rather than to what you are saying.

CHAPTER FOUR

VOICE PRODUCTION

31 By now you should have acquired sufficient skills for appreciation of sounds, an easy relaxation of the body and full breath control. You are thus prepared to study your voice, and we shall begin with the formation of the voice and its subsequent modification into good tone. We already know that the breath is the excitor for speech. Air acts as the excitor in many musical instruments; for instance in an accordion we have a bellows action (comparable with our rib action), by which the outgoing air in the accordion is made to vibrate, thus producing sounds, or more accurately, notes. With a bassoon, or an oboe, we use our breath as the excitor. The air is blown between two flat pieces of cane called a reed, which is placed between the lips. The breath causes the reed to vibrate and so produces a note. With a trumpet again, the excitor is our breath, but this time we vibrate our lips instead of a reed to produce the initial note. What is then the purpose of the trumpet's body?

The answer to this is the characteristic sound or **timbre** given to the initial note by the trumpet's shape. It also adds a ringing quality to the sound. Both these improvements in quality and amplification is a result of **resonance**. The trumpet's body is the **resonator**.

PHYSIOLOGY OF VOICE

32 Let us now further examine the process of sound formation. A sound occurs whenever something is set vibrating such as a plucked violin string, a struck piano wire, a beaten drum, a reed being blown and so on. Sound vibrations are of a **longitudinal nature**. Consider, for example, beating a gong. After the initial strike, the metal plate starts vibrating to and fro, which means that the air around the gong is alternately compressed and then rarified; squeezed or pushed and then relaxed is another way of putting it.

This regular push/pull action can be seen when the end of a long coil of wire is struck — the vibration travels along the coil in a concertina-like motion. It is almost like the action of a worm moving forward. Sound waves travel in this way through the air. When these waves hit the membrane of the ear, it, too, is set vibrating and the vibration excites nerves in the inner ear sending appropriate messages to the brain and that, very sketchily, is how we hear sounds. A similar process takes place in the human throat, where vocal cords act like a reed. The breath being forced between these cords sets them vibrating. The vibration is then passed on to the outgoing breath which now becomes voice.

33 THE VOCAL CORDS (often termed as **vocal folds**) are contained in a cartilaginous box positioned at the top of the trachea or wind pipe. You can feel this box with your fingers. It is called the **larynx** or more generally the voice box. The vocal cords are muscular in nature and stretch from the **thyroid cartilage** in front, where they are joined, to the **arytenoid cartilages** at the back. The sliding of the arytenoids causes the inner folds of the vocal cords to come together (see figure 4). When sufficient air is forced between the vocal cords in their closed position they begin vibrating very rapidly, and therefore to withstand the obvious strain, their inner edges are

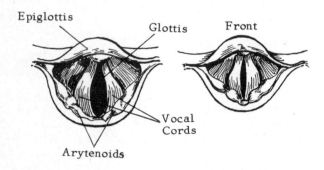

Fig. 4 Movements of the Vocal Cords

strengthened with additional tissue. These edges border the **glott**
glottal chink (see fig. 5).

Above the vocal cords is a pair of additional folds of muscular
tissue, the so called **false vocal cords**, which act as a protection for
the true vocal cords.

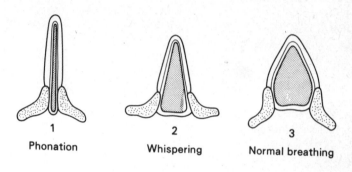

1	2	3
Phonation	Whispering	Normal breathing

Fig. 5 Variation of Glottis.

34 The specific nature of the vocal cords, their position and
degree of tension combined with the varying force of the outgoing
breath contribute to the strength and pitch of the note, that is its
height or its depth. The pitch of the voice with regard to the vocal
cords is dependent upon:—

(a) **the length** — the longer the cords, the lower the note and vice
versa.

(b) **the thickness or mass of muscular tissue** — the more weight
there is, the lower is the note.

(c) **the degree of tension** — the less the tension, the lower the
note.

(d) **the elasticity** — the greater the elasticity, the greater the
flexibility of notes produced.

The variation of the length and tension of the vocal cords is
controlled by the **intrinsic muscles** of the larynx. These help to tip

the arytenoids backwards, away from the thyroid, and also to move the thyroid forwards. It's by this co-ordinated action that the cords are stretched, made thinner and more tense, and so a higher pitch is produced. With regard to the pressure of the exhaled air, this also helps to determine the force or loudness of delivery, but an increase in pressure also usually results in a higher pitch.

Obviously, the workings of the larynx and vocal cords are very complex, when one considers the infinite number of variations concerning pitch and volume of the human voice.

35 THE LARYNX can be seen on figures 6-9, showing various views when stripped of its covering muscles — the **extrinsic muscles** of the larynx. The larynx is a slightly funnel-shaped structure of cartilage (gristle) held together by muscle and tissue. It is attached to the **hyoid bone** under the tongue by the **thyro-hyoid membrane.**

The larynx consists of a number of parts called cartilages. The largest is a shield-like cartilage, **the thyroid,** which forms the front of

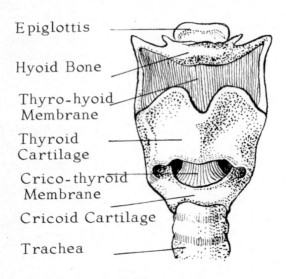

Fig. 6 Front view of larynx

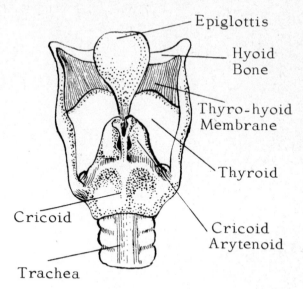

Epiglottis

Hyoid Bone

Thyro-hyoid Membrane

Thyroid

Cricoid Arytenoid

Cricoid

Trachea

Fig. 7 Back view of larynx

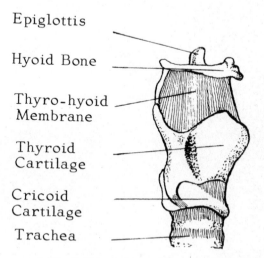

Epiglottis

Hyoid Bone

Thyro-hyoid Membrane

Thyroid Cartilage

Cricoid Cartilage

Trachea

Fig. 8 Side view of larynx

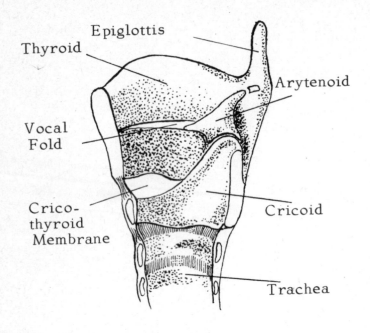

Fig. 9 Interior of right half of larynx

the larynx and extends on either side, but does not form a complete ring. At the base of the thyroid cartilage is another, shaped like a ring. This is the second largest cartilage in the larynx and is called the **cricoid**. It resembles a signet ring, being widened at the back. Below the cricoid cartilage is the trachea, composed of several incomplete rings of cartilage. They are open at the back to allow any particles accidentally entering the air passages to be ejected. The remaining gap at the back is sealed by the food pipe. Resting on the back part of the cricoid are two pyramid-shaped pieces of cartilage called the **arytenoids**. The arytenoids can perform a sliding side to side movement, to and from each other, and can also tip to and from the thyroid.

At the top of the larynx, just above the thyroid, is a protective cartilage which acts as a flap to open or close the entrance to the larynx. This is the **epiglottis**. Many people believe that its purpose is to close the entrance to the larynx, chiefly to prevent unwanted particles of food and drink getting into it. However, such protection is equally well secured by the rise of the whole of the larynx against the back of the tongue during swallowing. Modern outlook favours the idea that the function of the epiglottis is more to direct the air to and from the nose in conjunction with the soft palate.

As mentioned earlier, the outside of the larynx is encased in extrinsic muscles. These serve to pull the whole larynx downwards or to raise it towards the base of the tongue. The purpose of a downward movement of the larynx is to vary the size and shape of the cavity above the larynx, the throat.

It must be noted, however, that the above account of the structure of the larynx and its workings is purposely simplified to aid clarity.

RESONANCE

36 The note produced by the vibration of the vocal cords is further modified by the hollow cavities in the neck and head — **the resonators**. There are two important facts to remember about any resonators. Their effectiveness depends upon the size of a cavity and the size of its opening, the **orifice** as it is called.
Resonance is a sympathetic vibration. If you sing a note into a piano while the pedals have been released, you will notice that the note you sing is being reproduced by the appropriate piano string. Even the strings an octave above and an octave below vibrate. Certain other strings join in to contribute to the initial note. The result is a much fuller sound with added overtones, it is a pleasantly rich sound — a resonated sound.

Take an empty glass and hold its open end towards your mouth. Sing a note and pass the glass from side to side across the mouth. Each time the open end passes your mouth, you will hear that there is a sudden swelling of the sound. This is also due to resonance. A similar example of this effect is heard when speaking in a hollow room or in a cave. Even a bad singer can enjoy the resonance of his notes, achieved whilst singing in his bathroom, for example.

A similar echo effect, and consequent build-up of roundness of sound, also occurs in the cavities of the head and is the main prerequisite of good vocal tone. Tone is the quality or timbre of the voice and to obtain a good timbre, one must activate all parts of the mouth in achieving the desired resonance of the voice.

If you use an empty glass as a resonator and blow across its top, you will hear a certain note. If you pour in some water and repeat the action, the note will be higher. As more water is poured in, the note becomes higher and higher, thus illustrating that the size of the resonator determines the note. The smaller the cavity, the higher the note. The second important fact concerning the size of the entrance of a resonator — the orifice — can be demonstrated if you whisper **WOW**. Repeat this several times, looking in a mirror. Did you notice that, as the mouth opened wider, the pitch went higher? This confirms that the size of the orifice also modifies the note i.e. the larger the orifice, the higher the note.

THE HUMAN RESONATORS

37 **The Pharynx (throat). This lies just above the larynx and** extends up to the soft palate. Its muscular walls help to vary its shape. It is composed of three parts: the **laryngopharynx** — just above the larynx, the **oropharynx** — at the back of the mouth, and the **nasopharynx** — at the back of the nose.

The mouth. As with the pharynx, this resonator, too, can vary greatly both in size and shape. The shape of the roof of the mouth at the front is fixed by the rigid hard palate. The soft palate or **velum** can be raised into an arched position or lowered to meet the back of the tongue, in which position it closes the back of the mouth. The floor of the mouth is formed by the tongue, the most flexible organ of the body. Its movements greatly alter the shape of the mouth cavity. The orifice of the mouth resonator is bordered by the lips, movements of which can further enhance resonance.

The nose. This resonator has both a fixed size and shape. It is divided into two cavities by a bone called the **septum**. Towards the top on either side there are scroll-like bones called **turbinates**. The turbinates are partly hollow which accounts for their light weight. The fullest nasal resonance occurs when the velum is lowered, although some additional sympathetic vibration can be attained if the voice is correctly 'placed' on the hard plate. When this occurs, sound waves penetrate the hard palate — the same way as sound penetrates the walls of a house — and this causes resonance in the nose.

The sinuses. These are the hollow bones in the head. There is the **frontal sinus,** immediately behind the eyebrows; **the maxillary sinus,** beneath the projection of the cheek bones, and the **ethmoid** and **sphenoid** cells found near the lower orbits of the eyes. It is now generally believed that these cavities serve only to make the skeletal structure of the head lighter and hence not used much as resonators. However, as sounding boards they to aid tone quality. This becomes even more apparent when the sinuses are blocked or inflamed with mucus — the tone of the voice becomes deadened.

The chest (thorax). This has been purposely left to the end, because there is much controversy of opinion over whether the thorax can really be regarded as a resonator. The lungs occupy most of its space, and it would seem therefore, that we are considering a potential resonator which is full of sponges. Nevertheless, it is unlikely that we get chest resonance. The thorax only serves as a sounding board like the box beneath a tuning fork — the sound vibrations passing along its bones help to amplify the tone.

38 Good tone further depends upon a balance between the resonances in the pharynx, mouth and nose. In fact, the vocal sounds are essentially pure resonances, and each acquires its characteristic pitch by the co-ordinated actions of all the factors involved in these resonators — cavities in the mouth and throat, the size of the oral opening and the space between the tongue and palate.

RESONATOR SCALE

39 To determine what is called the resonator scale, one may begin with the vowel *oo* as in *hoot.* Here the mouth orifice is small, and so the pitch is a low one. The pitch in the mouth is in fact the same as that in the throat. If you whisper this vowel, you will hear the resonant pitch. Change the word into *hood* and notice a slight increase in the vowel pitch, because the mouth orifice has increased slightly. A simple progression in the height of the pitch will be heard

in the series of vowels occurring in *hoard, hot* and *hard.* Up to this point, the resonant pitch in both the mouth (that is in front of the tongue) and that in the throat (behind the tongue) is identical. After *hard,* the pitch of the mouth resonance continues to rise in the following series, whilst the throat resonance pitch decreases: *hut, heard, hat, head, hid* and *heat.* The explanation here is that the mouth orifice continues to increase in size and the mouth cavity decreases as the tongue rises at the front. At the same time, the cavity behind the humping of the tongue increases with the consequent lowering of the tone. Try whispering the vowels in this sequence and listen to the rise in pitch (two extra sounds are included to satisfy a musical scale, but in *hoe* and *hay* the vowels are double ones, although in singing only one sound may be produced): *hoot, hood, hoe, hoard, hot, hard, hut, heard, hat, head, hay, hid, heat.*

This account of the resonant scale is rather academic but by paying attention to the balance between the resonances in the throat and mouth a good tone will be produced on vowel sounds. Exercises on this are given on pages 45 and 46.

TONE FAULTS

40 Breathiness. Here the vocal cords are brought together too loosely, resulting in an escape of breath during vocalisation. Sometimes this can be caused by growths on the vocal bands, thus preventing their approximation. Lack of muscular vitality can also produce a slackness in the meeting of the vocal cords.

Care needs to be taken that not too much breath is allowed to escape on voiceless consonants, and that as soon as voiced consonants and vowels are spoken there is no wastage of unvocalised breath. Singing exercises will help here. Avoid allowing too long a delay between voiceless consonants and following vowels as in *park, fool,* start the vocalisation as soon as possible. Basically, the amount of breath for speech should be used more economically.

Stridency. This is a harsh, metallic quality in the tone caused by too much tension in the vocal mechanism and resonators. Particularly prominent in the production of this fault is the forcing together of the vocal cords and hence harsh noise is added to the fundamental note being produced. Stridency is also produced by emotional strain which produces tension in the throat and mouth. A pinched throat will certainly result in this fault, caused by strain on the speaker's part to project from the throat instead of from the diaphragm. The larynx is drawn up by extrinsic muscles towards the tongue bone or **hyoid**.

Improvement of breathing, followed by relaxation exercises, especially of the neck and larynx, will be necessary towards overcoming stridency. Take care to start vocalisation of vowels without a jerk or a glottic shock (see chapter 8).

Throaty tone. This is an unpleasant gutteral quality associated with the tone. The fault may be due to a fading of the breath control at the ends of phrases, resulting in the 'tone falling back' into the throat. This throatiness is also accentuated by having the tongue raised incorrectly in the mouth.

Thin tone. This is essentially a lack of balance between the mouth and throat resonance; there is too much of the former and not enough of the latter.

Nasal tone, nasal twang or nasality. This occurs when the control of the soft palate is slack. For all sounds in English except *m, n* and *ng,* the soft palate must be kept raised. If there is escape of sound down the nose on vowels, the tone has an unpleasant "talking down the nose" effect. The converse to nasality occurs when the nasal passages are blocked and *m, n,* and *ng* are heard as *b, d* and *g* respectively.

41 EXERCISES FOR GOOD TONAL PRODUCTION

(a) Start by taking a deep breath through the mouth and singing the vowel sounds heard in the words *hoot, hoard, hard, heard, heed.*

(b) Repeat exercise (a) starting quietly and gradually increasing volume to a crescendo, then conclude with a diminuendo or quietening.

(c) Intone the series — *hoo, hoe, haw, hah, her, hee.*

(d) Start with a big yawn. Follow this with singing *hah, hoo, hee.*

(e) Practise projecting *way, wee, wie, woe, woo.*

(f) Perform this figure eight exercise. Start with *mah, nah, lah;* then follow the arrows ending with *ah.*

This exercise can be repeated by using various other initial consonants such as *th* (as in *those*), *v* and *z.*

			mee	*nee*	*lee*			
may	*nay*	*lay*				*may*	*nay*	*lay*
			mah	*nah*	*lah*			
maw	*naw*	*law*				*maw*	*naw*	*law*
			moo	*noo*	*loo*			

(g)   Whisper *ah*, then add voice. Gradually change the vowel sound with no jerks to *ee* and then *oo*. This is called vowel blending. You can practise this exercise with all manner of vowel combinations.

(h)   Sing words such as *bell, boom, ding-dong, bang*. Start with plenty of attack on the *b* or *d* and then let the vowel ring out. Lengthen the final consonant.

(i)   Hum *m, n* and *ng*, feeling the vibration of sound in the nose. Repeat with variation of scales.

(j)   Sing the following sequence, dwelling on the sounds coming down the nose: *manning - menning - minning - monning - munning.*

(k)   Sing *ng* and gradually change to *ah*.

(l)   Practise projecting a part of the resonant scale with varying initial and final consonants such as the following:

1 — initial consonant exemplified as in

poo, poh, paw, pah, per, pay, pee
boo, boh, baw, bah, ber, bay, bee
too, toh, taw, tah, ter, tay, tee
doo, doh, daw, dah, der, day, dee

Repeat with initial *k, g, f, v, th, s, z, sh, m, n, l,* and r.

2 — final consonant exemplified as in
oop, ohp, awp, ahp, erp, ayp, eep
oob, ohb, awb, ahb, arb, ayb, eeb
Repeat with final consonants as shown above.

Constant practising with vowel sounds alone or combined with consonants will help you to acquire a good vocal tone.

CHAPTER FIVE

ARTICULATION

42 In chapter one we discussed the value of certain vowels and consonants to the ear. The consonants can produce sharp staccato effects, frictional sensations and musicality. Apart from these aesthetic qualities they have a very important function in speech since they are responsible for the framework of words and hence produce clarity of utterance.

If one takes a sentence such as *Get six people inside the taxi*, and repeats it, making sure that the consonants are accurately formed, while making every vowel the same, namely an *uh* sound (or neutral vowel, see chapter six), the sense of this sentence can still be conveyed: *guht-suhx-puhple-uhnsuhd-thuh-tuhxuh*. Try to convey the sense just by saying the vowels however accurately: *e-i-ee-uh-i-ie-uh-a-i*. It cannot be done. We can say therefore, that clarity of transmission depends on the accuracy of the formation of the consonants, or as we say, accuracy of articulation. Slovenly articulation makes speech incomprehensible.

43 Good articulation depends on five factors:

accuracy — which is achieved when the correct organs of articulation are used,

distinctness — largely dependent on the discrimination between vocal and aspirate consonants,

firmness — vital organic exertion given to consonants; there must be no slackness nor exaggeration,

fluency — neat transition from one consonant to the next without breaking the smooth flow of delivery,

deliberation — the comfortable choice of the rate of delivery in order to allow all the consonants their correct and easily recognisable formations.

Let us just illustrate those five facets of articulation from the adverse point of view, that is when each in turn is neglected. The sentence we will take is:

My father lives with my brother in an old attic.

Term neglected	Result
Accuracy	*My fahver lives wiv my bruvver in an ol a'i'*
Distinctness	*My father lifs with my brother in an olt attic.*
Firmness	*Ummy fatherrr lives withuh my brrrother in an olduh attic.*
Fluency	*My father/ lives with/ my brother in an/ old/ attic.* (/ = break in flow)
Deliberation	*My fatherlis wi my brother in a nol dattic.* (gabbled speech).

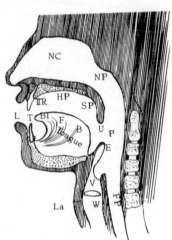

The organs of speech

NC - Nasal cavity
NP - Nasal passage
L - Lips
P - Pharynx
T - Teeth
Bl - Blade (of tongue)
F - Front (of tongue)
B - Back
E - Epiglottis
V - Vocal cords
FP - Food passage
W - Wind pipe
TR - Teeth ridge
HP - Hard palate
SP - Soft palate
U - Uvula
La - Larynx

Fig. 10 Side view of head

44 Obviously care has to be taken with the formation of the consonants in order to secure the articulation. For this purpose we must constantly practise exercises to sharpen all the organs of articulation. The organs of articulation are the lips, the teeth and gums, the hard palate (the front of the roof of the mouth) and the soft palate (the roof of the mouth at the back).

In figure 10 the organs of articulation are clearly labelled in a drawing of a side view of the head.

ORGANS OF ARTICULATION

45 THE LIPS are mobile, fleshy organs capable of being pushed forwards and drawn backwards, spread to the side or reduced to a small circle. In conjunction with the jaws they can form a wide circle. They can move independently, each being able to position itself behind one of the sets of teeth. In order to increase lip mobility, there are many exercises you can perform, and since the jaw also works closely with the lips and is very important for clarity and projection, we shall begin with flexibility exercises for the lips and then the jaw.

Lip Exercises
(a)   Push the lips forwards to make a tube shape, then spread them in a wide smile and finally open the jaws so that the lips form a large circle.
(b)   Repeat exercise (a) adding sound and making the movements smoothly so that *oo* blends into *ee* which blends into *ow*.
(c)   Spread the lips and curl them in and out in quick succession.
(d)   Lightly press the lips together and blow between them so that they vibrate.
(e)   Screw the lips up and move them from side to side.
(f)   Perform the following exercises rhythmically, emphasising all lip movements:
    pay – pee – pie – poh – poo.
    bay – bee – bie – boh – boo.
    Repeat with *w, m, f* and *v*.
(g)   Practise the following sentences feeling the firm movements of the lips on *p, b, w, m, f* and *v* sounds:
    Put a pound of peanut butter in the pan.
    Bounce the ball boldly off the blackboard.
    When will Willy wed Wendy?
    Mary's mother makes meringues every Monday.
    Freda's father fearlessly fought five ferocious foxes.
    Vera Vaughan visited Valerie in Vienna.

Jaw Exercises
(a)   Try to imitate a goldfish. Allow the jaw to drop under its own weight, then raise it to close the mouth (keep the tongue tucked inside). Repeat this slowly at first, and then speed up.

(b) Drop the jaw and swing it forwards and backwards, then swing it from side to side.

(c) Drop the jaw and gently rotate it.

(d) Keeping the lips tightly closed 'chew' an imaginary huge lump of gum.

(e) Say the following words, exphasising the mouth opening on the initial sound:

arm, ark, ask, art, aunt, ounce, out, ouch, odd, ox, eye, isle.

(f) Try saying these sentences feeling the opening of the jaw on the vowel sounds:

How odd of aunt Marjorie to walk past the bar.

'Ah' opens the oral opening admirably.

Ask Arthur to arrive at Oxford on time.

I came out of the cave alone.

I like almond tarts, apple pie and ice cream.

46 THE TONGUE is the most flexible organ in our body. It is capable of extremely rapid movements and can curl, twist, move out and in and side to side. The importance of improving tongue agility cannot be over-emphasised.

Tongue Exercises

(a) Flap the tongue against the top teeth rapidly.

(b) Scrape the tongue tip behind the bottom teeth as if you were trying to remove some toffee trapped there.

(c) Push the tongue out of the mouth, then curl the tongue tip up and down aiming to touch the nose and then the chin. Next, touch the right and left cheeks with the tongue tip.

(d) Drop the jaw and curl the tongue tip up and down inside the mouth.

(e) Curl the tongue into a "U" shape and push it through a small circle formed by the lips.

(f) Drop the jaw and make the tongue flat in the mouth. Practise raising first the back of the tongue and then the front. Check these movements by using a mirror.

(g) Let the tongue loll out completely relaxed, then tense the tongue into a point.

(h) Repeat the following exercises rhythmically:

tay -- tee – tie – toh – too

day – dee – die – doh – doo
then carry on with the *th* sounds, then *s, z, l, n, k, g* and *r*.

(i) Practise the following sentences, concentrating on the tongue movements:
Twist the twine tightly round the tree trunks.
Did Dora dare to deceive David deliberately?
Kate Cooney carefully closed the kitchen cupboards.
Gregory Garside gained good gradings in Greek grammar.
Naughty Nora has no nice neighbours.
Little Larry Lester lolled lazily on the Li-Lo.
Rosemary Wright was richly dressed in red corduroy.

47 THE SOFT PALATE forms the back of the roof of the mouth. This is capable of being lowered when the sounds *m, n* and *ng* are formed.

Soft Palate Exercises

(a) Sing *ah* and slowly change to singing *ng*. Watch what happens in the mouth by using a mirror.

(b) Repeat the following rhythmically:
ang – eng – ing – ong – ung (the last as in *hung*)
manning – menning – minning – monning – munning.
krangk – krengk – kringk – krongk – krungk.

(c) Practise the following sentences:
Many strong men were working down the mines.
During the long mornings the labouring increased.
Nancy Mannering was trying anxiously to ring her dancing partner concerning their performing in that evening's competition.

48 Having now exercised all the mobile organs of articulation, you should now proceed to the following exercises which involve the use of all the speech organs in many orders. Don't aim for speed, accuracy is far more important. The vowels printed are found in this sequence of words: *had, head, hid, hod, hut.*

Rhythmical Exercises

(a) *ap – ep – ip – op – up*

ab – eb – ib – ob – ub
at – et – it – ot – ut
ad – ed – id – od – ud
ak – ek – ik – ok – uk
ag – eg – ig – og – ug

(b) Stress the first syllable in each of the following nonsense words:

pappety – peppety – pippety – poppety – puppety
babbedy – bebbedy – bibbedy – bobbedy – bubbedy
tattety – tettety – tittety – tottety – tuttety
daddedy – deddedy – diddedy – doddedy – duddedy
kakkety – kekkety – kikkety – kokkety – kukkety
gaggedy – geggedy – giggedy – goggedy – guggedy

(c) Start off building up a sequence of consonants like this. Begin with *p - t - k*, say them stressing the *k* so that you produce a rhythm of a cantering horse. After a while add *b* so that the rhythm now becomes that of a train going along the old railway lines "clickety click". After this add in turn *d - l - f* and *g*, so the whole sequence is *p - t - k - b - d - l - f - g*. You can repeat this exercise with any combination of consonants you wish. Here are two more sequences for you to build up *t - l - p - g - v - y - r* and *f - l - p - r - w - d - g - v - y - z*. You will have to add a little *uh* sound after each of the voiced consonants to produce a flowing rhythm. When you are proficient, you can add the three sequences given above together.

Tongue Twisters

49 There are many rhythmical exercises which you can devise for yourself. To conclude this section on sharpening the articulation, here is a selection of tongue twisters collected from various sources. Practise the short ones at least three times each.

Truly rural.
Peggy Babcock.
Red leather, yellow leather.
Unique New York.
Fresh fried fish.
A cracked cricket critic.
Mixed biscuits.

Abominable abdominal.

Try tying twine round the three tree twigs.

The seething sea ceaseth and thus sufficeth us.

Imagine an imaginary menagerie.

She sat upon a balcony inexplicably mimicking him hiccuping and amicably welcoming him in.

Theophilus Thistle, the successful thistle sifter, in sifting a sieve full of unsifted thistles, thrust three thousand thistles through the thick of his thumb.

CLASSIFICATION OF CONSONANTS

50 Now that the exercises for articulation have been covered, we must turn to the more fundamental aspects of the consonants, namely their formation and classification. The alphabet contains twenty one consonant letters, which are used when printing or writing words. However, when speaking, we use at least twenty four different consonant sounds in standard English (other sounds are added in various parts of the British Isles).

This discrepancy becomes even more apparent when we consider the number of vowel letters (five) and the number of vowel sounds we use (see later). To use ordinary letters for denoting the value of the surplus number of sounds would present problems and necessitate lengthy explanations, let alone the risk of confusion.

This risk is being minimised by the use of accepted phonetic symbols. Each of these symbols represents a distinct speech sound called a **phoneme**. For instance, the phonemes which are spelt in the following words by the letters *ch* are quite different from each other: *machine, stomach, chop*. These differences are accurately represented by phonetic symbols / ʃ /, / k /, / tʃ / respectively. Whenever phonetics are used, these symbols are isolated from the rest of the text by two oblique strokes, one preceding and one following the phonetic transcription.

With the majority of the consonants, the phonetic symbols used are identical with the letters of the alphabet, eg. / p, b, t, d, k, g, f, v, s, z, l, .r, w, h /. The following symbols, however, have no equivalence with the alphabet and should therefore be learnt:

/ θ /	– as in *thin*,	/ ð /	– as in *this*,
/ ʃ /	– as in *shoe*,	/ ʒ /	– as in *rouge*,

/ ŋ /	– as in *ring*,	/ j /	– as in *yell*,
/ tʃ /	– as in *chip*,	/ dʒ /	– as in *just*.

Rarer examples used mainly in Scotland are / ʍ / heard in *white*, and / x / as heard in *loch*.

51 For classification purposes three considerations must be made concerning each consonant sound:

(a)   place of articulation,
(b)   manner of articulation,
(c)   vocalisation.

PLACE OF ARTICULATION

52 To decide this, consideration must be given to the speech organs used in the formation of the consonant and its description is then derived from the names of these organs. For example:

Organs used	Examples	Description
lip + lip	/ p, b, m, w, ʍ /	bi-labial
lip + teeth	/ f, v, /	labio-dental
tongue + teeth	/ θ, ð, /	lingua-dental
tongue + teeth ridge	/ t, d, n, r, l, s, z, /	alveolar
tongue + hard palate + teeth ridge	/ ʃ, ʒ, /	palato-alveolar
tongue + hard palate	/ j /	palatal
back of tongue + soft palate	/ k, g, ŋ, /	velar
vocal cords	/ h /	glottal

MANNER OF ARTICULATION

This refers to whether the consonant is formed by:
(i)   a complete oral stoppage of the breath flow followed by a sudden release, eg. / p, b, t, d, k, g, /. These are called **plosive consonants.**

(ii)   a complete oral stoppage followed by a gradual release, eg. / tʃ, dʒ /. These are the **affricates**.

(iii)   a complete oral stoppage with the consonant sound emitted down the nose, eg. / m, n, ŋ /. These are the **nasals**.

(iv)   a spasmodic oral stoppage, eg. / r / called the **flapped** or **rolled R**.

(v)   a partial oral stopage, eg. / l /. the lateral consonant.

(vi)   a narrowing in the oral cavity to cause friction, eg. / f, v, θ, ð, s, z, ʃ, ʒ, /. These are the **fricatives**.

(vii)   no oral stoppage or friction, eg. / j, w /. These are called **frictionless glides**.

VOCALISATION

Consonants are formed either with breath alone or with vocalised breath. The former are called **aspirate** or **voiceless consonants** eg / p, t, k, f, θ, s, ʃ, x, tʃ, h /. The latter are **voiced consonants**, eg. / b, d, g, w, v, ð, z, ʒ, m, n, ŋ, l, r, j, d /. Phoneticians use the term **fortis** for the voiceless and the term **lenis** for the voiced consonants. Fortis means strong and the aspirate consonants are indeed made with greater muscular effort than the voiced ones, which are therefore termed lenis meaning weak.

The table on the next page summarises the classification of the consonants.

53 We shall now take each consonant in turn and notice its classification, the phonetic symbol used and special features (if any). Practice is then given in words and sentences for each sound.

P   bi-labial plosive aspirate / p / (figure 11)
Here the lips are brought together and suddenly parted. No voice is heard. As with all plosives, there is a positioning of the organs of articulation, a slight pause and then the release of the sound. Note that / p / before a vowel sound has a slight / h / sound added to it to avoid a hard initial attack.

Practise: *pin, power, paw, slipper, sloppy, nip, rope, hiccough.*
Patrick was a popular chap because he was dapper and spread happiness.

Table No. 1 CONSONANT CLASSIFICATION TABLE

manner of articulation and duration

Place of Articulation	complete oral closure — plosives	complete oral closure — affricates	nasals	spasmodic — flap	partial — lateral	narrowing — fricatives	glides — semi-vowels	Vocalisation
bi-labial (two lips)	p / b		m			ʍ	w	aspirate / voiced
labio-dental (lip & Teeth)						f / v		aspirate / voiced
lingua-dental (tongue between teeth)						θ / ð		aspirate / voiced
alveolar (tongue and alveolar ridge)	t / d		n		l ɫ	s / z		aspirate / voiced
post-alveolar (tongue behind alveolar ridge)		tɹ / dɹ		r				aspirate / voiced
palato-alveolar (tongue with sides of hard palate & alveolar ridge)		tʃ / dʒ				ʃ / ʒ		aspirate / voiced
palatal (tongue and hard palate)						ç / ʝ	j	aspirate / voiced
velar (back of tongue and soft palate)	k / g		ŋ			x		aspirate / voiced
glottal (vocal cords)	ʔ					h		aspirate / voiced

Put the packet of peas in the pot ready for the preparation of the soup.

Possibly Paul and Peter prefer a plate of porridge to a portion of pasta for supper,

N.B: p is silent in pneumonia, receipt, coup, cupboard, jumped, pseudo-, psycho-, psalm.

B   bi-labial, plosive, voiced / b / (figure 11)

Formed as / p /, the released breath carries the voice.

Practise: bob, bib, bat, rubber, lobby, obtain, grubby, about, drably, grab.

Barbara bought a bit of best butter and a basket of bilberries.

The brigadier bellowed bravely as the big bombs blasted about him.

Bring the rubber plants into the shrubbery, Betty.

N.B: b is silent in limb, lamb, thumb, comb, debt, subtle, doubt.

T   alveolar, plosive, aspirate / t / (figure 12)

Here the consonant is made by the meeting of the tip of the tongue with the alveolar ridge, and the rim of the tongue with the side teeth. No voice is heard.

Note that *-ed* after voiceless consonants becomes / t /, eg *jumped, looked, locked, laughed, guessed, whipped.* However, this rule does not apply after *t* or *d,* eg. *totted, noted, dreaded;* other exceptions are *wicked* and *naked.*

Practise: *tax, tin, tome, pottery, matter, stack, tots, Thames, mast.*
The Tuesday night's tennis team won the tournament.
Try tickling the tip of the terrier's snout.
Timothy Tucker stole two tins of tested tomatoes.
N.B: t is silent in ballet, bouquet, castle, Christmas, fasten, glisten, whistle, rustle.

D   alveolar, plosive voiced / d / (figure 12)

Formed as / t /, the released breath carries the voice.

After voiced consonants *-ed* becomes / d / eg. *dragged, robbed, loved, burned.* Sometimes *-ed* has syllabic value, eg. *beloved.*

Practise: *day, dose, dud, madly, gladden, saddest, candle, wider, pods.*
The adventures of Donald Duck delighted the doctor's eldest daughter Dorinda.

Dennis was told not to dawdle on the road.
Daisy Dodding's driving was definitely dangerous.
N.B: d is silent in *Windsor, handsome, handkerchief.*

K   velar, plosive, aspirate / k / (figure 13)

The back of the tongue meets the soft palate. No voice is heard.

Practise: *kite, kill, skip, sink, tack, accuse, act, quart, antique, chemist, liquor, quay, lacquer. Note all those spellings for / k /.*
Kate cooked a creamy coffee cake for the county contest.
Can the cleaner come in and clear away the cocoa cups.
Clarissa Crawshaw cried continuously all through the competition at King's College.
N.B: k is silent in *knew, knit, knife, knee, knot,* and the printed *c* is not sounded in *muscle.*

G   velar, plosive, voiced / g / (figure 13)

Formed as for / k /. The released breath carries the voice.

Practise: *grow, gag, sag, dagger, ghost, guard, guilt, disguise, fatigue, intrigue.*
The gangster flogged the gagged man till he sagged and fell to the ground.
Gordon gave a grimace as he glanced at Grace snuggling into the green rug.
Garry gloomily gazed into the glass of gargle.
N.B: The *g* is not heard in *gnat, gnaw, diaphragm, sign, reign, Magdalen.*

CH   alveolar, affricate, aspirate / tʃ / (figure 14)

This composite consonant is formed by the tip, blade and rims of the tongue stopping the breath flow as they meet the alveolar ridge and side teeth. At the same time the tongue is raised towards the hard palate in readiness for the fricative / ʃ /. The stopped or plosive / t / is released slowly, allowing the breath to escape in a diffuse manner over the central surface of the tongue with friction occurring between the front regions of the tongue and the hard palate.

Note that when two affricates occur together, care must be taken to pronounce both, eg. *which chair, Dutch cheese, watch chain.*

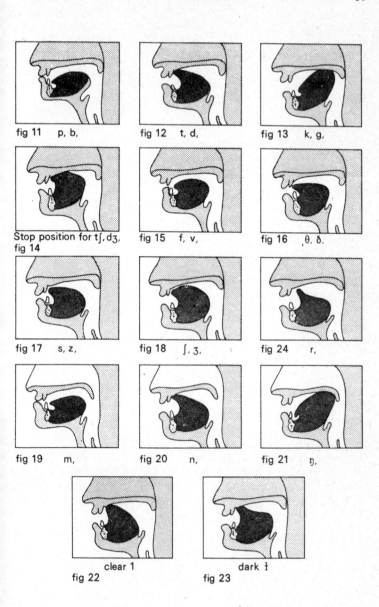

fig 11   p, b,

fig 12   t, d,

fig 13   k, g,

Stop position for tʃ, dʒ, fig 14

fig 15   f, v,

fig 16   θ, ð,

fig 17   s, z,

fig 18   ʃ, ʒ,

fig 24   r,

fig 19   m,

fig 20   n,

fig 21   ŋ,

clear 1   fig 22

dark ɫ   fig 23

Practise: *chair, choke, match, nature, question, mischief, posture, lecture.*
Charles's children ate rich cheese cakes rather than cheap chips from choice.
The Chelsea supporters cheered their champions with sheer delight.
Rachel Church chose cheerfully to venture into Chile.

J   alveolar, affricate, voiced / d ʒ / (figure 14)

The formation of this affricate is the same as for / tʃ / but, of course, it is vocalised. Again care must be taken when two affricates come together as in *large jar, Judge Jeffreys.*

Practise: *gin, jest, midget, suggest, adjacent, avenge, soldier, Belgian, ridge, gauge, grandeur.*
George jerked every joint as he was jumping in the gymnasium.
Judge Jefferson journeyed jauntily from Jamaica to Jersey.
The ridge jutted out just above the soldiers' heads.

TR – DR   post-alveolar fricatives / tɹ / – / dɹ /

The centre of the tongue is hollowed ready for the R type friction. The release of the stop is slow – compared with the fast plosive released of t and d in / tʃ / and / dʒ /.

Practise: *tree, trick, trap, poetry, entrance (noun or verb), dream, drab, dreary, address, taudry.*
Andrew and Tracy were entranced by natural history.
'Tis strange but true; for truth is always strange, stranger than fiction.
Audrey tried to drive the dray cart through the country lanes.

F   labio-dental fricative aspirate / f / (figure 15)

Note that when / f / is the final consonant in a singular noun, it frequently becomes / vz / in the plural form eg. *thief, thieves; leaf, leaves; loaf, loaves; shelf, shelves.*
    The sound changes to / v / when a verb is derived from a noun ending in *f* eg. *thief, to thieve; shelf, to shelve.*

Practise: *fork, fun, off, stuff, physics, enough, soft, swift, giraffe, telephone, cough, laugh, lieutenant.*
Frances fell forward with full force against the fireplace.
Fenella's friend Fanny foolishly formed funny faces.
Philip flew to and fro for his frequent visits to France.

V   labio-dental fricative voiced / v / (figure 15)

Practise: *vim, veal, have, review, curve, of, Stephen, nephew.*
The valleys of Venezuela were very vast.
Veronica viewed the vendetta with venom.
Vicky revived the violets by her valiant fervour.

TH   lingua-dental, fricative aspirate / θ / (figure 16)
Plurals and verbs derived from singular nouns take the voiced TH in
many cases, eg. *bath, baths, to bathe; mouth, mouths, to mouth;
path, paths; breath, to breathe; teeth, to teethe.*

Practise: *thief, thought, both, athlete, worthless, length.*
The growths were measured in sixths of an inch, not eighths.
If the three free threads are red, Fred, thread the free three threads.
The thick thistle sticks were every third and fourth in the series.

DH   lingua-dental fricative voiced / ð / (figure 16)

Practise: *there, this, those, breathe, loathe.*
The brothers loathed the smothering ways of their mother.
The mother soothed the baby with teething trouble.
*With solemn oaths and muttered truths, the wreaths were laid on the
paths.*

S   alveolar fricative aspirate / s / (figure 17)
This, together with Z is known as a hissing sound or a sibilant.
S frequently becomes / z / after final vowels and after voiced
consonants eg. *as, is, his, hers, theirs, yours, beads, burns, breathes.*

Some exceptions: *yes, this, thus, us,* and *bus.*

Practise: *sat, cease, sample, pass, niece, science, axe, gasps, rents,
grievance.*
Stella sealed the sachets securely.
*Stuart slowly perceived the solemnity and seriousness of the
situation.*
The peace talks were progressing satisfactorily.
N.B: s is silent in aisle, isle, island, viscount, debris.

Z   alveolar fricative voiced / z / (figure 17)

Practise: *zoo, zeal, prize, frozen, dessert, dissolve, poses, scissors,
desert, reserve, blizzard, ease, raise.*

The houses in the resort were deserted because of the disastrous blizzard.
The zoo was full of lions and tigers and bears.
The Zulu chieftains made zig-zag patterns on the hides of their animals.

SH alveolar fricative aspirate / ʃ / (figure 18)

Practise: *shoe, ship, machine, schedule, sure, assure, ration, mansion, mission, conscience, special, ocean, luxury.*
Sheila's precious stones were shut up in the show case.
She always wore fashionable shoes and a shawl when she went shopping.
The dishwashing machine was insured with the Providential Assurance Society.

ZH alveolar fricative voiced / ʒ / (figure 18)

Practise: *vision, measure, leisure, beige, azure, transition, garage, prestige, rouge.*
Jeanne, my gorgeous French maid, is a vision with her azure eyes and reddest of rouged cheeks.
To gain pleasure, measure your leisure time carefully.
The pigeons added to the confusion as they became camouflaged against the beige garage door.

H glottal fricative aspirate / h /

Sometimes with words such as *had, have, he, him, has, his, who* in unstressed positions in a sentence, the initial / h / is dropped, eg. *Tom has gone out, I gave her a book.*

Occasionally / h / is added to an initial W sound when the bilabial fricative aspirate is heard / ʍ / as in *white, whirled, whale.*

Practise: *heat, hand, home, how, ahead, behave, perhaps, behind, anyhow.*
Harry abhorred to hold hands with his hateful Henrietta.
Heliotrope handkerchiefs were hardly high fashion.
Who hopes to have a house on Hampstead Heath?
N.B: The *h* sound is not heard in *heir, heiress, honest, honour, hour, annihilate, vehicle, shepherd.*

THE NASALS

In contrast to the plosives which are oral stops, the nasals *m, n* and *ng* are produced by the vocalised breath flow escaping through the nose, by the lowering of the soft palate or velum, whilst there is some stoppage of the breath in the mouth.

M bi-labial nasal sustained voiced / m / (figure 19)

In rapid speech / m / frequently takes the place of / n / before a following bi-labial. eg.

> *one mile* becomes *wummile*
> *more and more* becomes *more ammore*
> *ten pence* becomes *tempence*

However, in careful speech it is quite possible to distinguish the / n / and the following bi-labial, and the above slovenly habits must be avoided.

Note the syllabic nature of / m / in *prism, rhythm, chasm.*

Practise: *meat, mix, drummer, comb, autumn, roaming, amongst, lumber, empty, firms, prompts.*
Many men make much money mining minerals.
Mime and movement make up most of the drama classes on Monday nights.
Mary Morrison married Michael Maloney in Manchester last March.
N.B: *m* is silent in *mnemonic.*

N alveolar nasal sustained voiced / n / (figure 20)

Here the tongue forms a closure with the teeth ridge and upper side teeth as for / t / and / d /.

Often, after plosive consonants, *-en* or *-on* assumes syllabic value eg. *happen, mutton, kitten, cotton, trodden, sodden, ridden, sicken, organ, often.* This also occurs sometimes after fricatives eg. *southern, listen, fasten, mission, dozen, vision.*

To handle the syllabic / n / the plosive consonant is positioned in the mouth, but not released. The / n / is then released down the nose. With the fricative the two are blended together but more pressure is given to / n / as it is released through the nose.

Practise: *now, many, men, meant, thunder, funny, banner, know, gnat, sign, pneumatic, snout, walnut, amnesty, earthen.*
Nancy never wandered on the mountains alone at night.
Norman's nightly nightmares began to numb his mind.

Nellie's nanny never neglected to admonish her for untruths.
N.B: n is silent in autumn, solemn, column, condemn, hymn, damn.

NG   velar nasal sustained voiced / ŋ / (figure 21)
The closure is formed with the back of the tongue and the lowered soft palate. Care should be taken that no / g / or / k / is added to / ŋ / especially when it is followed by a vowel, eg. *singing out, swinging away, flying off, bring out.* To handle this, lengthen the / ŋ / and lift the note of the vowel a shade.

Sometimes of course, / k / or / g / is heard after / ŋ /, eg. *sink, drank, slunk, longer, finger, linger, wrangle, strangle, nightingale.*

Practise: *sung, long, uncle, anxious, anxiety, anchor, banquet, distinguish, enquiry.*
The young monk was singing the wrong song.
Morning and evening the training was being carried out in the hangar.
The anchor sank into the shimmering water.

L   alveolar lateral sustained voiced / l / (figures 22 and 23).
This sound, as with the nasals / m /, / n /, / ŋ / is capable of inflection. These four sounds, together with R are sonorous and help to produce the music of speech. Compare *well* as a question and as a summing up exclamation, the tune is quite different. As are the tunes in *That is all!* and *Is that all?*

There are three variations to this sound, the first is the voiceless form which is not usual in standard English but is met with in Welsh, eg. *Llandudno, Llewellyn,* etc. It can occur to some extent after a voiceless consonant, notably / p / and / k / eg. *clear, plate.* More important for our purposes are what are called **allophonic variations**. These refer to slight variations in the position of the organs of articulation which result in a quality change in / l / and yet the sounds are still clearly recognisable as / l /. These two forms are known as clear and dark L.

The clear L is formed when the tongue tip is raised to the upper teeth ridge and the sound escapes over the sides of the tongue, i.e. laterally. There is a front vowel quality about this L sound, almost like the *ee* in *see.* (see chapter six). The clear / l / occurs before vowels and before / j /. It can also occur finally in a word when followed by a vowel in the same phrase, eg. *well off.*

Practise: *lip, let, lamp, climb, blow, glum, yellow, collect, million, failure, value, sailing, sail in, fall out, all over.*
Lily laughed loud and long.
Silly Billy fell over the lamp flex.

The dark L represented by the symbol /ɫ/ is formed when the tongue tip touches the teeth ridge and the sound escapes laterally, but the difference from the clear /ɫ/ is that /l/ has a back vowel quality roughly that of *u* in *put.* (see chapter six). The dark /ɫ/ occurs after a vowel in a word ending a phrase, before a consonant and when it has syllabic value. Note that it is pronounced in: *alter, fault, halt, salt, false, almost, balcony, alternative, also.*

A long /l/ is heard in the following: *palely, shrilly, stalely, vilely, solely, wholly;* and also when a final /l/ and an initial /l/ meet, eg. *I'll leave, we'll let you know, Paul listens.*

Practise: *call, feel, till, help, field, milk, elbow, faltering, subtle, rattle, nettle, apple, stable, little, cuddle, fickle, eagle, camel, tonal, squirrel, awful, weasel, uncle, wrangle.*
The old shelves needed to be altered to accommodate all the piles of books kept on the hall table.
Little by little the oil trickled almost to the edge of the vale.
N.B: This consonant is not sounded in the following: *almond, calm, palm, halve, could, would, should, talk, walk, salmon, folk.*

R   alveolar sustained voiced / r / (figure 24)

This consonant has several forms. In standard English we have the flapped R, which is the commonest form. Here the tongue tip is either held near to, but not touching the upper teeth ridge or it may be raised momentarily to the same position. The soft palate is raised. The back rims of the tongue are touching the upper molars, the central part of the tongue is lowered to produce a hollow effect. There is no friction and the sound is allowed to escape over the central part of the tongue. Examples of this type of R are heard in: *read, rest, rat, marry, very, far away, Westminster Abbey.* This flapped R is also heard after consonants except / t / and / d / eg. *free, throw, belfry, crow, mushroom.*

After / t / and / d / another form of R is heard, this is the fricative / ɹ / and with / t / and / d / forms affricates. Here the tongue tip produces friction with the rear part of the alveolar ridge eg. *true, tripe, drive, drink.*

A devoiced form of R is heard when it follows the aspirate consonants / p, t, k / as in: *press, pray, tray, crease, acrue.* This mainly occurs when the plosives are accented.

A rolled R is not usual in standard English, but is heard in Scotland. This is produced by a rapid succession of taps by the tip of the tongue on the alveolar ridge.

Another variation or **an allophone** of R is produced by using the back of the tongue against the soft palate. This is the uvular R and is common with French people.

The R in English is only pronounced when it is followed by a pronounceable vowel in the same phrase. Let us note some examples of that statement. R would be pronounced in the following: *raw apples, put the car away, fairy lights, take care of him;* but it would not be heard in: *Is that the car? It's fair. Take care. It's hard. Are you warm?* It is not heard either between vowels, eg. *china ornaments, law and order, I saw it,* etc.

Practise: *rip, rage, road, diary, carry, mirror, express, attract, dread, write, rhythm, rhyme, rhinoceros.*
Roger and Ruth tramped and trudged their weary way through the marshy woods.
The library looked literally littered with contemporary literature.
The temporary secretary progressed well in February but deteriorated in April.

THE SEMI-VOWELS. This term applies to / w / and / j / because when used as consonants, they have vowel-like qualities approximating to / u: / as in *who* and / i: / as in *heed,* respectively.

Y lingua-palatal semi-vowel sustained voiced / j /
Here the tongue begins in a position for the vowel / i: / as in *tea* and quickly glides to the shape required by the following vowel. Try holding the sound / i: / for a moment and then shift to / u: / as in *who,* the result will be *you* written phonetically / ju: /.

Practise: *yes, yawn, young, unite, Europe, pew, tune, huge, queue, onion.*
The Duke yearned for the view from the dunes.
Do you voyage in your yacht every year?
The yokel produced a beautiful tune from his new lute.

W bi-labio-velar semi-vowel sustained voiced / w /.

This is formed by rounding the lips and starting with a back vowel / u: / (hence the use of the term velar). The vowel quickly glides to the following vowel. Form / u: / as in *who* and then shift to / i: / as in *heat*, the result will be / wi: /.

The letter A can represent three different qualities when preceded by / w /. Compare the following: *walk, wall, war, warm, water; wander, want, wasp, quarrel, swan; wag, waggon, wax, whack, quack.*

Practise: *will, warp, when, whither, language, persuade, suite, one, once; squash, quilt, choir.*
We will wait for Willy for a wee while.
When will the Queen be persuaded to wear her jewels?
Wendy awoke with a weird feeling she was being watched by twelve witches.

N.B. w is silent in: *sword, wrap, wreck, write, who, whose, whom, whole.*

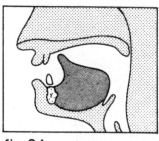

fig 24   r,

CHAPTER SIX

THE SINGLE VOWELS

54 A vowel is a sound which is emitted through a free opening of the mouth. It is not stopped or hindered by the organs of articulation.

There are many different vowel sounds, we say each has a different quality. The vowel quality is determined by the positions of the lips and tongue. If these positions do not alter in the production of a vowel, we have a **monophthong** or simple or single vowel. When there are two positions of the articulatory organs, we have a **diphthong** or a double vowel. With three positions we have a **triphthong**.

In the following passages we shall deal with the twelve monophthongs.

THE MONOPHTHONGS

55 Vowels are described and classified with reference to the shape of the lips and the position of the tongue. The lips may have different degrees of spreading but are never forced into a smile, they may be held loosely in a circle called the neutral position, they may be openly rounded or closely rounded into a tiny circle. The tongue can be raised at the front, in the middle or at the back. The degree to which the tongue is raised is described by reference to four positions. These are called **close, half-close, half-open** and **open**. The close and open terms refer to the highest and lowest positions assumed by a particular part of the tongue.

The distance between the close and open positions is divided into three. When the tongue is raised two-thirds of this distance, it is in the half close position; when only raised one-third, it is in the half-open position. The tongue may be tensed or relaxed (called lax). The tongue tip is always behind the bottom teeth for vowel production and the soft palate is always kept raised. Besides the description of the tongue and lip positions, mention can be made of the duration of the vowels, but as you will see, this can vary according to the consonants following the vowel in question.

For instance, the vowel in *cat* is traditionally shorter than that in *car*, but in words such as *cad* and *cast*, the duration could easily be reversed. However, it is convenient to refer to the monophthongs as short and long.

56 Let us now study the twelve monophthongs in detail. As with the consonants, the phonetic symbol and description of formation will be given. A list of common spellings follows, and the words given should be spoken for vowel practice. Say all the words aloud and think about the sound formation. In this way you will learn the theoretical aspect of each vowel. Finally, there are a few sentences for you to practise.

From time to time, exercises involving comparisons between vowels to help improve ear training have been introduced. Wherever necessary, comments concerning special features of the vowel, exceptions or variations in pronunciation are added and attention is drawn to difficult articulation.

57 The five long monophthongs are heard in this sentence:

Heat soon forms firm plants.

The seven short monophthongs are heard in this sentence:

That leather is not much good.

The diagram on the next page represents where and how far the tongue is raised when making the above twelve vowels. Each word given appears in the diagram at its appropriate place; *leather*, of course, has been separated into its two parts *leath* and *er*.

EE as in HEED / i: /

The front of the tongue is raised to almost close position, it is tense and the side rims make contact with the upper molars. The lips are neutral. It is a long monophthong.

Common spellings. Note the following various spellings of this sound and say the words aloud. Follow this by saying the practise sentences aloud and finally compare any words given which help you

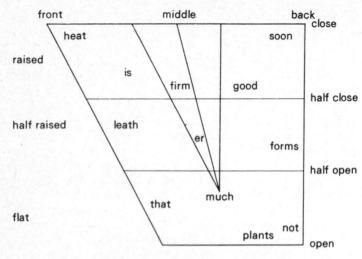

Fig. 25 Tongue positions for monothongs.

to distinguish one vowel from another. Repeat this procedure for all the vowels given in this chapter.

e   as in stressed positions particularly before vowels for example:
      be, he, she, we, me, also the first syllable in *Eden* and usually
      in *these, epoch, complete, penal*

ee   as in *free, see, bee, cheese, queen, beef, tree, eel*

ea   as in *east, beat, plea, team, stream, leaves, reach, peace,
      breathe*

ie   as in *brief, thieves, piece, chief, niece, believe*

ei   as in *ceiling, seize, receive, conceive, seizure, sheik*

i   as in *machine, suite, police, caprice, fatigue*

Rarer spellings. ey as in *key;* **eo** as in *people;* **ay** as in *quay;* **oe** as in *Oedipus;* **eau** as in *Beauchamp.*

Practise reading these sentences aloud:
The Queen was sweetly dressed in leaf green.
The cheese seemed too heated to eat as a treat.
Jean seems to breathe with a wheeze when she sleeps deeply.
The meal was pleasing and started with steamed eels and was completed by peaches and cream.

l as in HID / l /

A short monophthong formed with the front of the tongue raised to just above the half-close position, it is lax and the side rims make contact with the upper molars. The lips are neutral.

Common spellings. As before, say the following words and sentences aloud, noting the various spellings; also practise the comparisons given at the end of the sentences. By practising comparisons appreciation is developed in distinguishing between various vowel sounds.

i   as in *wit, sixth, risk, imp, chip, with*
y   as in *city, wordy, stocky, gymnastics, murky, happy*
e   as in *pretty, noses, roses, exact, pleaded, relax, cement*
ie   as in *cities, posies, ladies, caddies*
a   as in *private, village*

Rarer spellings

ui   as in *built, biscuit*
u   as in *business*
ee   as in *Greenwich, coffee, toffee*
ay   as in *Monday,* etc.
o   as in *women*

Practise the following sentences *aloud:*

Which witch switched the switches?
Little Miss Smith is still sick.
Jill will still bring in the milk for the twins.
"Nip a bit of the thick, crisp biscuit, Nicky".

Now we can start comparisons. Firstly hear the difference in duration of the vowels when followed by a voiced and then a voiceless consonant. What difference do you hear? Hold your larynx to determine what is happening.

bead – beat	*thieve – thief*	*bid – bit*
heed – heat	*sieze – cease*	*hid – hit*
need – neat	*rib – rip*	*lived – lift*

Determine the distinction in vowel quality between the following pairs of words which should be said aloud:

feel – fill	*least – list*	*reach – rich*
seek – sick	*seen – sin*	*bead – bid*
keen – kin	*leak – lick*	*sheep – ship*

Can you hear any difference when those vowels occur before the consonant L? Say the following series aloud:

sin – sill – seal	*fin – fill – feel*
win – will – wheel	*pin – pill – peel*
kin – kill – keel	*gin – gill – congeal*

E as in HEAD / e /

This is a short monophthong, the front of the tongue is between half-open and half-close, it is more tense than for / I / and the side rims make light contact with the upper molars. The lips are neutral.

Common spellings

e   as in *egg, hen, swell, fetch, knelt, bell*
ea   as in *dread, head, heather, meant, cleanse*
a   as in *Thames, many, any,*

Rarer spellings

ei   as in *leisure*
ue   as in *guest*
eo   as in *leopard*
ieu   as in *lieutenant*
ie   as in *friend*
u   as in *bury*
ai   as in *again*

Practise reading the following sentences aloud:
When will the weather get better?
Get Fred to check the next set of red thread.
Ben pretends to be a friend but I suspect he is a deadly enemy.
Red cherries make the very best jellies.

A as in HAD / æ /

This is a short monophthong. The mouth is slightly more open than for / e /. The front of the tongue is raised just below the half-open position and is tenser than for / e /, the side rims make very light contact with the upper molars. The lips are neutral, that is loosely open.

Common spellings

a   as in *hat, chat, rat, sack, flat, match, rash*

Rarer spellings
ai   as in *plaid, plait*
al   as in *salmon, scalp*

Practise the following sentences aloud:
It was romantic when fans were in fashion.
We must attack the camp with our tanks.
Clash, clang, clatter, batter, bash and bang – a rhythm of destruction, catch it if you can.
Patsy and Sally are happy paddling and splashing about in the water tank at the back of their caravan.

Once more we start comparisons, appreciating the duration of the vowels and the change in qualities. Say the following aloud:

Duration	Qualities
bed – bet	*seed – Sid – said – sad*
led – bet	*deed – did – dead – dad*
send – sent	*heed – hid – head – had*
bend – bent	*lead – lid – led – lad*
bag – back	*reek – rick - wreck – wrack*

Can you hear any slight changes in vowel quality when / e / and / æ / are followed by the L sound?

ten, tell; fen, fell; when, well; pan, pal; man, Mall.

U as in HUT / ʌ /

This short monopthong is formed when the centre of the tongue is raised slightly above the open position and there is no contact with the upper molars. The jaws are open and the lips are neutral and relaxed.

Common spellings
u   as in *bun, just, drudge, bus, gull, sun, hush*
o   as in *son, won, done, month, other, tongue*
ou   as in *young, couple. enough, country, touch*

Rarer spellings
oo   as in *blood, flood*
oe   as in *does*

Practise the following sentences aloud:
It's fun to have buttered currant buns for supper.

He won tons of lovely money with his brother.
Mother can't understand the fun of trudging over the rough country.
Sunday lunch is rather fun, with onions and duck, sponge with custard and rum punch.

AH as in HARD / ɑː /

This is a long monophthong. The tongue is almost flat i.e. the open position, and there is no contact with the upper molars. The jaws are open wide and the lips neutrally open and relaxed.

Common spellings

a	as in *bath, past, father, vase, chance, glass*
ar	as in *car, tar, farther, arm, art, bark*
ear	as in *hearth, heart*
al	as in *almond, balm, half, calm, palm, qualms*
er	as in *Berkshire, clerk, Hertford*
au	as in *aunt, draught, laugh*

Practise the following sentences aloud:
Father started to gargle with a glass of brandy.
The shark started to gasp as the lance parted his heart.
Her aunt cast a glance at the passing guards.
Charles Arthur Darnley, Master of Arts, carved the facade on Marble Arch.

O as in HOT / ɒ /

This is a short monophthong. The back of the tongue is in the fully open position and there is no contact with the upper molars. The jaws are wide open and there is slight lip rounding. Send the sound forward and avoid any dampening by the soft palate.

Common spellings

o	as in *hot, strong, jog, wrong, thong, knock*
a	as in *what, watch, quantity, wrath, swan, squad*
au	as in *because, laurel, sausage, Austria, quarrel*

Rarer spellings

ow	as in *knowledge*
ou	as in *cough, trough*
ach	as in *yacht*

Practise the following sentences aloud:
John trod on the box which involved a lot of cost.
Hobbling along, the cobbler fobbed off the mockery of the jostling mob.

The quarrel was over the quantity not the quality of the hot chocolate.
Don tossed rocks into the long rotten log box.

AW as in HOARD / ɒː /

This is a long monophthong. The back of the tongue is raised between the half-open and half-close position and there is no contact with the upper molars. The lips have medium rounding.

Common spellings. When practising this sound, take care that the tip of the tongue does not rise from its natural vowel position behind the bottom teeth. No conscious R sound should be heard. Be on the look out for some traps in ensuing sentences where the R is printed but is not heard in standard English.

or	as in *torn, sword, lord, fork, bore, torn, corn*
aw	as in *saw, law, yawn, lawn, saw, pawn*
al	as in *stalk, walk, chalk, talk*
ar	as in *war, quart*

Rarer spellings

a	as in *water*
au	as in *daughter, cause*
oor	as in *floor, door*
oar	as in *board, coarse*
ore	as in *bore, chore*
our	as in *court, four*
oa	as in *broad*

Start making your own lists of words containing the same vowel quality, but represented by various letter spellings.
Practise the following sentences aloud:
Audrey and Maud were bored, they yawned and walked out of the laundry.
Claud's daughter caused a storm by mauling a courtier on the lawn.
Nora Vaughan always wore tawdry baubles.
Sean bought an awful portion of prawns.

U as in HOOD / ʊ /

This is a short monophthong. The tongue is raised towards the back to just above the half-close position. There is no contact between the tongue and the upper molars and it is a lax vowel. The lips are rounded.

Common spellings

u   as in *put, sugar, pulpit, bull*
o   as in *woman, wolf*
oo   as in *good, foot, rook, soot*
ou   as in *should, would, could*

Rarer spelling: or as in *worsted.*
Practise the following aloud:
It was understood that you wouldn't, not that you couldn't.
The cook put too much sugar in the pudding.

OO as in HOOT / u: /

This is a long monophthong. The back of the tongue is raised to the close position and is tense. There is no contact with the upper molars. The lips are forward and closely rounded.

Common spellings

oo   as in *fool, cool, moon, soon, loose*
o   as in *who, do, lose*
ou   as in *coupon, soup, through*

Rarer spellings

u   as in *rude*
ue   as in *true*
oe   as in *shoe*
ew   as in *threw*
ui   as in *sluice*

Practise the following sentences aloud:
It was against the school rules to let loose balloons.
The goose got loose and flew and slew the rooster.
You may choose fruit spoons or soup spoons.
He was doomed to clean boots and shoes in the gloomy room.

Apart from the examples given of / u: / above, the sound very often occurs preceded by / j / to form the sound / ju: /. Care must be taken when this combination is preceded by / t / or / d / that / j / is not dropped or we have *choon* for *tune* and *juke* for *Duke*.

Practise these words containing / ju: / and then proceed to the sentences:
new, muse, few, hue, argument, cube, mule, beauty, costume, tune, dune, tulip, Tudor, Duke, stew, tube, astute.

The Duke reviewed the troops as the bugle sounded.

The new pewter ewers look beautiful when used with the tulips or fuchsia.
There was a huge queue to book for the new revue which opens on Tuesday.
June knew it was her duty to tell Judy she was neurotic.

We can now make some more comparisons. Say the following lists aloud and listen to the effect on a particular vowel as the consonant following it changes. Listen also to any change in the choice of vowel purely for the sake of comparison. Try isolating the vowel from the word:

bud, but; bug, buck; mug, muck; card, cart; hard, heart; halve, half; fob, fop; dog, dock; rod, rot; awed, ought; sword, sort; board, bought; good, foot; pull, put; brood, brute; lose, loose; use (verb), use (noun); rude, root; nude, newt; abuse (verb), abuse (noun).
bead, bid, bed, bad, bud, barred, bod, bored, Buddha, booed; cat, cut, cart, cot, caught, coot; peat, pit, pet, pat, putt, part, pot, port, put.

ER as in HEARD / ɜː /

This is a long monophthong. The centre of the tongue is raised between half-close and half-open with no contact with the upper molars. The lips are neutral.

Common spellings

er   as in *her, fern, serve, berth, mermaid*
ir   as in *first, stir, shirk, bird*
ear   as in *yearn, learn, heard*
ur   as in *urn, turn, churn, occur*
or   as in *word, work, worm*
our   as in *journey, adjourn, courtesy*
eur   as in *saboteur, masseur, connoisseur*

Rarer spellings

yr   as in *Myrtle*
urr   as in *purr*
err   as in *err*
olo   as in *colonel*

Practise the following sentences aloud:
Myrtle yearns to sell shirts, jerseys and skirts.
Mr. Earnshaw searched the earth for a circular church.
The earl was an amateur concerning the worth of pearls, but was a

connoisseur of certain liqueurs.
It was irksome of the herd to lurch all over the newly turned earth.

THE NEUTRAL VOWEL / ə /

This is a short monophthong. The tongue is raised to almost half-way in the centre between half-open and half-close, the degree of raising depends to some extent according to its position in the mouth. The lips are in a neutral position. The neutral vowel has the commonest occurrence of any vowel in the English language. It always occurs in a non-stressed or unaccented position. The use of the neutral vowel aids the natural rhythm of delivery and helps to avoid stilted pedantic speech.

Various Forms of Spelling

Rather than list all possible combinations, which would take up a lot of space, below is given a list of words illustrating many of the spellings of the neutral vowel. In multi-syllabic words we have underlined where the neutral vowel occurs.

China, absurd, above, sofa, linen, gentlemen, brother, baker, moment, possible, oblige, obstruct, concern, conclude, submerge, labour, stubborn, cupboard, steward, pleasure, nature, tortoise, precious, figure, toughest, restless, kindness.

Many monosyllabic words have two pronunciations which are called the strong and weak forms. The weak form occurs in an unstressed position in a sentence and often has the neutral vowel. Some examples of words using the neutral vowel in an unaccented position are as follows:

a, an, am, and, are, as, at, but, can, could, do, does, for, from, had, has, have, must, of, or, saint, shall, should, some, than, that, the, there, them, to, was, were, would.

Make up sentences containing these words in an unstressed position.

Reading practice

Rosemary was unable to accept the present of a set of saucepans from the gentleman whom she met, when she was travelling home from Ascot on the excursion train, and who engaged her in conversation concerning cookery. (23 neutral vowels).
I told him that that, that that student offered to the convention, was absurd and inaccurate from all considerations. (14 neutral vowels).

CHAPTER SEVEN

THE COMPOUND VOWELS

58 The compound vowels are made up of either two monophthongs which form a **diphthong**, or two monophthongs plus the neutral vowel, which is termed a **triphthong**. The individual members of the diphthong or triphthong glide into each other by movements of the tongue and lips. Usually the stress and length in a diphthong occurs on the first vowel and hence such diphthongs are called **falling diphthongs**. There are eight diphthongs, three of which end in the neutral vowel and are termed **murmur diphthongs** or **centring diphthongs**. There were other terms used to describe diphthongs, such as "vanish" and "true". The former referred to those diphthongs composed of two short monophthongs as in the words *hate* and *hoe,* and the latter to the diphthongs made up of a long and a short monophthong as in *kite, coy,* and *cow.* Recent work has shown that these classifications are too rigid; for instance, compare *gaze* with *grace:* the first component in *gaze* is longer than that in *grace.* Hence the former is not made up of two identically short monophthongs.

THE DIPHTHONGS

59 The description of diphthongs is more accurate by describing the glide travelled from the initial to the final vowel. Of course, there are many variations in the starting and final positions when individual people are studied. This is what makes the diphthongs the culprits in speech. Variations in the qualities of these vowels, the **allophonic variations** as they are called, produce differences in regional accents. They also present difficulties to overseas students. In this chapter we shall study the initial and final positions of each compound vowel. Those positions have been given in chapter six. When practising the diphthongs and triphthongs, start with the initial vowel and glide to the final vowel by thinking of that final

sound. As with the monophthongs the various spellings of each sound together with any special features will be given. Then follows sound practice and comparisons.

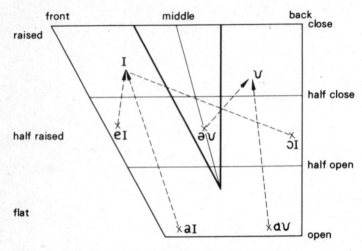

Fig. 26 Tongue glides for the falling dipthongs.

AY as in SAY / eɪ /

See figure 26. A falling diphthong composed of / e / and / I /. During the execution of this vowel the jaw closes slightly and the lips are neutral.

Common spellings

a	as in *fate, take, lady, lazy, bass*
ay	as in *play, ray, say, day*
ai	as in *plain, stain, fail, trail*
ei	as in *weight, reign, eight, feign*

Rarer spellings

ey	as in *grey, they*
al	as in *halfpenny*
ao	as in *gaol*
au	as in *gauge*

Practise the following sentences aloud:
Jane bathed the baby each day in a grey pail.

Hazel Yates waits in vain for the late train.
May placed the eight cakes on the plate next to the tray of dates.
The shape of the maple and hazel trees made a change to the plain.

I as in SIGH / aɪ /

A falling diphthong composed of / æ / and / I /. Actually the tongue
starts in a position slightly lower than / æ / but for our purposes
/ æ / will suffice. The glide is bigger than for / eɪ /, the closing
movement of the jaw being more evident.

Common spellings

i   as in *dice, mine, fine, white*
y   as in *try, sly, why, fly, scythe*
igh   as in *might, tight, flight, sight*
eigh   as in *sleight, height*
ie   as in *lie, died, pie*

Rarer spellings

ei   as in *either*
uy   as in *buy*
aye   as in *aye*
ye   as in *rye, dye*
eye   as in *eye*
ai   as in *aisle*

Practise the following sentences aloud:
Simon admired Ida's eyes which he said reminded him of sapphires.
Ivy decided that the final nicety would be lime trifle.
Brian fell on his thigh after trying to ride his bicycle on the ice.
"Hermione is quite the right type", said Diana with a smile.

Both these diphthongs are longer before a voiced consonant (lenis)
than before an aspirate (fortis).

Compare these words aloud noting both the duration and changes
of quality.

*made, mate; aid, eight; graze, grace; hide, height; eyes, ice; ride,
write; fete, fight; play, ply; rate, right.*

Hear the effect on the vowels when followed by a dark l: *mail, sail,
grail, while, still, mild.*

OY as in COY / ɔɪ /

This is a falling diphthong composed of / ɒ / and / I / the tongue movement is therefore from back to the front. The lips change from round to neutral.

Common spellings

oy   as in *boy, joy, toy, coy, oyster*
oi   as in *choice, voice, boil, coin*

Rare spelling

uoy as in *buoy*

Practise the following sentences aloud:
Joyce's noisy voice annoyed Roy Lloyd.
What noise annoys a noisy oyster?
The boys got great joy from their new toy destroyers.

OH as in SO / əʊ /

This falling diphthong starts with the neutral vowel and proceeds to / ʊ /. There is a slight closing of the jaw. The lips change from neutral to slight rounding.

Common spellings

o   as in *no, old, bolster, mope, soda*
oa   as in *roam, foam, oak, loathe*
oe   as in *doe, toe, roe, hoe*
ow   as in *low, know, slow, mow*
ou   as in *though, mould, soul*

Rarer spellings

au   as in *mauve*
eau as in *plateau*
ew   as in *Shrewsbury, sew*
oo   as in *brooch*
eo   as in *yeoman*

Practise the following sentences aloud:
Joan's cold composure froze Joe's devoted moping as she showed him home.
Joseph Stone sold the rogues loads of old gold.
The robe was mostly of a noble tone of mauve and was cut low over the shoulder.
The old crone spoke her oath below the broken oak.

OW as in HOW / ɑʊ /

A falling diphthong starting with / ɑː / and gliding to / ʊ /, although

the slight rise of the tongue is a fraction more forward than for
/ ɑː /. The glide is more extensive than for / əʊ /. The lips start with
a neutral open position and end with being weakly rounded.

Common spellings
ou   as in *mouse, house, found, ground, sound*
ow   as in *how, now, brown, cow, allow*

Rarer spellings
ough as in *bough, plough*
ao   as in *Maori*

Practise the following sentences aloud:
The crowd, being roused by coward's howls, shouted loudly.
The stout count allowed the crowds around his house and grounds.
Howard Browning was a bounder endowed with a proud brow but a
loud mouth.
Our dog Towser growled at the prowler crouching under the couch.

Now say these short lists aloud to appreciate the change of duration
and quality. Note also the effect of a final dark / ɫ /.

joys, Joyce; robe, rope; road, wrote; hosed, host; found, fount;
to mouth, a mouth; boy, bow (a ribbon), bough; boil, bowl, bowel;
coil, coal, cowl.

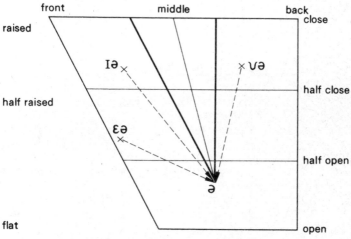

Fig. 27 Tongue positions for the centring dipthongs.

THE CENTRING DIPHTHONGS
as in *pier* / ɪə / *pair* / ɛə / *poor* / ʊə /

60 These diphthongs are made up respectively of / ɪ /, / ɛ / and / ʊ / followed by the neutral vowel. Take care that no ·/ j / is introduced between the elements in / ɪə / and / ɛə /, and that no / w / occurs in / ʊə /.

Selected spellings

/ ɪə /	eer	as in *cheer, beer, peer*
	ear	as in *fear, dear, rear*
	ere	as in *here, mere, sere*
	eir	as in *weird, weir*
	ier	as in *bier, pier, fierce*
	ir	as in *fakir*
	ea	as in *idea*
	ia	as in *India*
	eu	as in *museum*

/ ɛə /	are	as in *dare, hare, rare*
	air	as in *flair, chair, pair*
	ear	as in *wear, bear, tear* (verb)
	eir	as in *heir, their*
	ere	as in *there*
	ar	as in *scarce*
	a	as in *Mary, Sarah, precarious*

/ ʊə /	oor	as in *poor, boor, moor*
	ure	as in *pure, sure, cure*
	ur	as in *during, jury, mural*
	ewer	as in *fewer*
	our	as in *tour, amour, gourmand, gourmet*
	ue	as in *fluency*
	ua	as in *truant*

SENTENCE PRACTICE

/ ɪə /   *I fear that you were not clear when you said "what year?" it appeared like "what cheer!"*
The weird atmosphere in the rear of the theatre was eerie.
Be of good cheer, the beer here is clear.

/ ɛə /   *Beware of glaring, swearing, and staring at the proletariat.*
Take care you do not share a chair with a hairy bear.

/ ʊə /   *I'm sure that the numerous detours around Drury Lane are
infuriating.
Muriel was furious with the insurance she was offered on
the luxurious murals and miniatures which she assured were
not spurious.*

THE TRIPHTHONGS

61 The first five diphthongs described in this chapter (that is
excluding the centring or murmur diphthongs), may be followed by
the neutral vowel / ə /. In this way triphthongs are formed. The
triphthongs may be contained within one word or even between a
final diphthong of one word and a following neutral vowel in the
next word, eg. *lay about,* /eI ə /. The formation of the triphthongs
can be appreciated by reference in preceding sections to the
individual vowels of which each is composed. Thus we distinguish
the following five variations:

1. / eI ə /   as in *conveyor, ratepayer, slayer*
2. / aIə /   as in *fire, spire, buyer, byre, choir, diary, dryer, higher*
3. / ɔIə /   as in *employer, lawyer*
4. / əuə /   as in *mower, sower, Noah, lower*
5. / auə /   as in *our, flour, flower, coward.*

For each variation practise the following sentences aloud:
1. *The surveyor studied the greyer layers of the clay as it passed
along the conveyor belt.*
2. *Isaiah was fired with desire to make the spires higher. The buyer
required iron wires for a trial.*
3. *His employer, who was a lawyer, could never be a destroyer of
the truth.*
4. *Old Noah, the rose grower, has become slower as the mower of
the lower lawns.*
5. *The showers refreshed the flowers in our bower.
For an hour he scoured the tower for the coward.*

The vowel sounds are impossible to convey on paper. In order to
perfect them, guidance has to be given by a qualified teacher. All
one can do in a book such as this is to indicate the technical
formations and give examples for you to practise. Occasionally one
is asked to classify vowels in words and for this purpose see the
simplified table number 2, which will be useful for examination
purposes.

N.B. Place the actual letter or letters representing the vowel sound to be classified before its phonetic symbol in column 1 of the table 2, and then proceed with its classification as indicated thereafter.

Table No. 2   VOWEL CLASSIFICATION TABLE

Phonetic Symbol	Key word	Type	Lip position	Tongue position
iː	heed	long monophthong	neutral	front raised
ɪ	hid	short monophthong	neutral	front raised
e	head	short monophthong	neutral	front half raised
æ	had	short monophthong	neutral	front slightly raised
ʌ	hut	short monophthong	neutral	central slightly raised
ɑː	hard	long monophthong	neutral	almost flat
ɒ	hot	short monophthong	slightly rounding	flat
ɔː	hoard	long monophthong	medium rounding	back half raised
ʊ	hood	short monophthong	rounded	back raised
uː	hoot	long monophthong	closely rounded	back raised
ɜː	heard	long monophthong	neutral	centre half raised
ə	above	short monophthong	neutral	centre half raised
eɪ	say	falling diphthong	neutral	front half raised to raised
aɪ	sigh	falling diphthong	neutral	front almost flat to raised
ɔɪ	coy	falling diphthong	open rounded to neutral	back slightly raised to front
əʊ	so	falling diphthong	neutral to rounded	flat to back raised
aʊ	how	falling diphthong	neutral to rounded	flat to back raised

VOWEL CLASSIFICATION TABLE – *Continued*

ɪə	pier	centring diphthong	neutral	front raised to centre half raised
ɛə	pear	centring diphthong	neutral	front half raised to centre half raised
ʊə	poor	centring diphthong	loosley rounded to neutral	back raised to centre half raised
eɪə	layer	triphthong	neutral	front half raised to raised then to centre half raised
aɪə	higher	triphthong	neutral	front flat to raised then to centre half raised
ɔɪə	employer	triphthong	loosely rounded to neutral	back slightly raised to front then to centre half raised
əʊə	lower	triphthong	neutral to rounded to neutral	centre half raised to back then to centre half raised
aʊə	our	triphthong	neutral to rounded to neutral	flat to back raised then to centre half raised

CHAPTER EIGHT

SPEECH FAULTS

62 Accuracy in speech is the result of the correct formation of vowels and consonants together with observation of the accepted pronunciation of words, which demands the correct accentuation and appropriate choice of speech sounds. There should also be clarity, fluency and projection in order to ensure that the substance of the words spoken is transmitted to the listeners. There are many pitfalls in speech of which one must be aware. These have been listed in this chapter so that you may have a logical approach to the subject.

63 The first group of errors which are prevalent may be termed: substitutions, distortions, omissions and additions or intrusions.

SUBSTITUTIONS. As the name suggests, one sound is substituted erroneously for another. Under this heading we have the very common devoicing, especially of final vocalised consonants. The printed s, **th** and **f** are the usual culprits, but of course, several other consonants are often devoiced when they should have received full vocalisation. Practise saying the following sentences observing the vocalisations required which are underlined.

The cheeses of Wales are choice.
Lots of bees made music with their humming.
These substances are dangerous.
Mary's scissors were made of steel

DISTORTIONS. These can be vowel substitutions as in the case of *'die'* for *day*, *'toim'* for *time*, *'flah'* for *flower* and so on; or they may be affectations where again the vowels are distorted to satisfy the whim of the speaker who, through ignorance or mis-guidance, feels compelled to produce artificial utterance of such words, as: *'agayn'* for *again*, *'nayce'* for *nice*, *'involve'* for *involve* and the rest of the contrived pronunciations.

OMISSIONS. These occur when consonants, or in some cases whole syllables are dropped. Usually the final consonants are in jeopardy, and we get *'It's hoh'* for *It's hot,* *'Let's hie'* for *Let's hide,* etc., also *'libry'* for *library,* *'contempry'* for *contemporary,* *'withs'* for *widths,* *'lenths'* for *lengths,* *'six'* for *sixth,* *'hop back'* for *hopped back,* *'trip up'* for *tripped up,* *'nex top'* for *next stop,* *'lass station'* for *last station,* *'Artic'* for *Arctic,* *'Febry'* for *February,* *'reconise'* for *recognise* and many more.

ADDITIONS. Here extra vowels and consonants are added to words thus marring the accuracy of pronunciation: *k* or *g* is often added to *ng* and we have *ring + g* for *ring,* *something + k* for *something.*

Sometimes *p* or *b* is added after *m* or *t* or *d* after *n.* Examples are *sumpthing* for *something,* *luntsh* for *lunch.*

Vowels have been introduced in such words as *lovely (loverly),* *Westminster (Westminister),* *grievous (grievious),* *tumbling (tumberling).*

Consonants have been added to words, as in *cross* which becomes *crosst,* *drowned* which becomes *drownded,* *once (wunst),* *escape (excape).*

64 INTRUSIVE CONSONANTS. Here we have the insertion of a surplus consonant in between two vowels in the same phrase. The most notorious intrusive consonants are *r,* *w* and *y,* although in some cases *t* and *h* crop up in slovenly utterance.

INTRUSIVE r usually occurs between two neutral vowels or often after aw / ɔː / preceding another vowel. To avoid the intrusive *r,* one must realise that the tongue tip has to remain behind the bottom teeth during the vowel junction. One can also help the purity of formation by singing the vowel confluence. Practise saying the following phrases, observing the trap of the intrusive *r* which has been underlined.

The idea of the India Office's offering law and order is awe inspiring.
I saw Freda and Sarah at the drama academy.

Find out for yourself where the trap occurs in the following:
China and India are areas of vast population.
My father-in-law is drawing all the day.
I saw all the china ornaments.

INTRUSIVE *w* is really an exaggeration of the final part of the diphthongs oh / əʊ / and ow / ɑʊ /, or the lip rounding vowels / ʊ / and / u: / when followed by another vowel, so that a forceful bi-labial is heard. As with the intrusive *r*, two sentences have indication where intrusive *w* could occur, the rest are left for your investigation. To help avoidance of intrusive *w*, don't allow the lips to come together too much.

It is not so easy to all who are eager to improve.
How awful to owe Arthur all that money.
To Amy, who is always in my thoughts.
I had no idea how inaccurate it was.
The atmosphere was too awful and so eerie.

INTRUSIVE *y* usually occurs where / ɪ /, / i: / or / aɪ / occurs before a vowel.

My eyes have seen, my ears have heard.
Do you see all the old elm trees?
My idea was to plant the oak trees in the open ground.
The apple pie was better than the orange tart.
Try often to see if the operation can be effective.

Sometimes other consonants are introduced incorrectly, for instance *h* is mis-placed:
I honestly think hAlice hought to hopen the windows.

T sometimes intrudes between *n* and *sh* / nʃ /, *n* and *s* / ns / and *l* and *s* / ls /, as in words *bunch, crunch, lunch, inch, prince, dunce, once, waltz, else.*

GLOTTIC SHOCK is a jerk of the glottis caused by a forceful meeting of the vocal folds producing a cough-like effect. It occurs usually before vowels, either initially in a phrase or between a consonant and a vowel in the same phrase or even before a vowel in a multi-syllabic word. Occasionally the glottic shock substitutes for a plosive consonant. The symbol used to indicate a glottal stop is /ʔ/ Here it is used to indicate glottic shock and examples of all the occurrences cited above are given in the following sentences:

ʔActuaʔlly ʔEmily ʔought to coʔoperate.
Cockneys would often distort *I bought a little bottle* to *I boughʔa liʔle boʔle.*

It is difficult to erradicate the glottic shock, but it is very necessary because its use produces jerky, inelegant speech and constant occurrence of it can be harmful to the vocal folds. Aim for a smooth juncture between consonants and vowels and between vowels and vowels. Singing the junctures can be of value, but the main principle to follow is to avoid any stoppage in the larynx. This is not too difficult with sustained consonants before vowels and between two vowels, when the vocalised air stream can be maintained. More taxing is when a plosive consonant precedes a vowel. Here concentration must be devoted to the release of the plosive **in the mouth** and not in the larynx. At all costs avoid the forced jerk of sound before vowels.

Practise the following sentences, paying particular attention to a smooth juncture before vowels. The glottic shocks which could occur have been underlined in the first two sentences only.

My mother's eyes were almost azure.
To ask Amy is not the same as asking Enid.
The Shah is often ill; so is his aide.
Almost all the avocados were over-ripe.
Raw opium is of course illegal to import.

66 REDUPLICATED AND ALLIED CONSONANTS. The former occur in pairs of words where the final consonant of the first word is identical to the initial consonant of the second. With allied consonants the situation is similar, though only the organic formation is identical, the duration or vocalisation is different. The following examples give clearer illustration of these definitions:

reduplicated		**allied**
ripe pears	*save Vienna*	*rhubarb pie*
grab both	*kiss Sarah*	*hot dogs*
hot tea	*bees zoom*	*red tie*
bad dog	*both things*	*black gloves*
black cat	*with these*	*some boys*
big girl	*some money*	*ten days*
tough fight	*fine night*	*bad news*

These consonantal combinations can offer slovenly speakers a variety of speech faults. Firstly the consonant at the end of the first word may be dropped altogether thus changing *red deer* to *redeer* and *third term* to *thirterm*.

Alternatively the two consonants may be joined with a neutral vowel, thus changing *June night* into *June-er-night* and *old town* into *old-er-town.*

Pedantic speakers split the two words completely, thus destroying the fluency of the phrase; each consonant being articulated separately.

To control reduplicated and allied consonants we must consider basically the duration of the consonants conceived. If we are dealing with plosives as in *red tie,* the *d* should be positioned in the mouth but not released (think of making it but do not let it out). The *t* is then released with more pressure than usual after a short pause. The listeners will register the first consonant even though it has not been released. Practise the examples given above containing this combination of plosive consonants.

When we deal with sustained consonants, we simply lengthen the juncture between the two words but add extra pressure towards the end, eg. *some mothers* become *sommothers,* the first *m* being positioned and blended into the second which receives more force.

Here are a few sentences for you to practise. They include some traps outlined in preceding paragraphs:

The last train was at a bad time for the late trippers.
We hadn't time to ask Clarence to the annual lunch.
The top part of the currant tart is not as spicy as the filling
The sand dunes undulated down to where the waves softly lapped on the shore.
Some miles of venturing into the interior resulted in our coming across the big game.

67 REBOUND. This is the addition of a neutral vowel after the final consonant resulting in *baduh* for *bad, save-uh* for *save* and so on. To avoid this rebound in words ending with plosives, one must take care that there is no release of vocalised sound after the plosion has been completed. For words ending with vocal continuants the technique is to produce the vocalised consonant and then remove the vocal quality to result in the devoiced counterpart. To illustrate this, consider the words *cars* and *weave.* Phonologically these words end in / z / and / v / respectively; to avoid rebound, / s / is added to *cars* after / z / has been formed. In the case of *weave* / f / is added after / v / has been made.

68 When the dark *l* occurs, take care that it is not made over-dark by introducing a glottic shock or even a neutral vowel before it, so that *pale* becomes *pa?le* or *pay-uhl*, similarly *field* should not be spoken as *fee-uhld*. Don't allow the centre of the tongue to drop too much.

Sometimes / l / is substituted for / r / in such words as *very, fried rice* and *pray* which become *velly, flied lice* and *play*. This fault is prevalent amongst the Asiatics, particularly Orientals and is called **lambdacism.**

Practise curling the tip of the tongue up and down to avoid this fault.

FAULTY JUNCTURES

69 Very often junctures are badly handled and a final consonant is allowed to become too attached to the initial vowel in the next word, eg. *town owl* becomes *tow nowl; not at all* becomes *no ta tall*. To handle this type of juncture one has to reduce the pressure on the final consonant of the first word and then raise the pitch slightly of the initial vowel of the second word.

See if you can distinguish between the following pairs of words. Listen to the force of the vowels and consonants at the junctures. Study the pitch changes and degree of aspiration of the plosives:

I scream – *ice cream*
that's tough – *that stuff*
fine night – *finite*
a name – *an aim*
my ears – *my years*

70 Finally, by way of revision of chapters five and six, remember to be on the look out for, and to avoid these miscellaneous faults:

(a) Substitution of *ch* / tʃ / and *j* / dʒ / for *tu* / tj / and *du* / dj / in such words as *Tuesday, tumult, tune, tunic, tulip* and *duke, dune, dupe, dew*.
(b) Adding a fricative to *t* and *k* so that *time* becomes *tsime* and *kiss* becomes *kxiss* (x is the Scottish *ch* as in *loch*). Aim to separate the organs of articulation quickly after the formation of *t* and *k*.

(c) Failing to observe where the neutral vowel occurs.

(d) Putting the neutral vowel into what should be lateral or nasal plosion. In other words failing to produce syllabic *l*, *n* or *m*. Remember these words and how they are uttered: *little, fickle, sudden, mutton,* etc.

(e) Hammering consonants, that is the over-explosion after the positioning of plosive consonants.

Whenever you come across slovenly articulation in others, keep a record of what you hear and try to find out the reason why the fault occurred.

Make a list of commonly mis-pronounced words — words which are given distorted sounds, mis-placed accentuation and inaccurate numbers of syllables.

CHAPTER NINE

VOCAL EXPRESSION

71 The human voice is capable of an infinite combination of tunes and notes, force and rate variations, and tonal changes. All these contribute to an exciting prospect for the actor, public speaker, recitalist and conversationalist. A tremendous amount of experimentation can be carried out in exploring the voice, and realising the possibilities of a wide range of expressions revealing vitality and personality, but sight must never be lost of the fact, that the vocal expressions used should be directed to conveying the sense of what is being spoken. Mere concentration on vocal variety will render the speaker voice-conscious, and the words uttered will be a string of artificially embroidered sounds. On the other hand, a flat, monotonous delivery will obviously draw attention to itself and hence stultify the transmission. So there must be a balance between the sense and the sound.

THE MAIN VOCAL FACETS

72 There are six main facets of vocal expression: **pitch, pace, power, pause, inflection** and **tone**. As an easy technique to remember these, think of the word *pit* as if spoken with a stutter, thus providing a suitable abbreviation *P-P-P-PIT,* whereby each letter would stand for one important aspect of speech variety. Discussion will now follow concerning the nature and use of each from both the technical and artistic viewpoints.

73 PITCH. This is the placing of the voice on the vocal scale. One has as many pitches as notes in the compass of the voice. For convenience one can say there are three main pitch bands — the upper, middle and lower, but remember that within each pitch band there are many other pitch levels, eg. extremely high, extremely low and so on.

Explore your pitch range with the following exercises:

(a) Find your middle note by starting to sing EE / i: / from a very high note to a very low note. You should be able to have a compass of two octaves. Use a piano to check this. The note which is roughly situated between the two extremes of pitch is your middle or centre note. All the following exercises should start on this middle note, unless otherwise stated.

(b) From the middle note count upwards from one to eight, raising the note each time. Follow this by counting to fifteen lowering the note each time. Finally, proceed to count upwards to eight arriving at your original middle note.

(c) Take words such as *Oh, no, yes, good,* say each of them on your middle note, then go up one note in scale and repeat the words. Carry on practising this exercise until you reach your upper pitch limit; then come down your pitch range note by note – do not slide down. Determine your lowest pitch.

Various Uses of Pitch

There are several technical uses of change of pitch concerning either accentuation, emphasis, a change of thought or an emotional involvement. Let us have a closer look at each:

Accentuation. Most multi-syllabic words receive prominence on one or more of their component syllables. One way to produce correct accentuation on a word is to change the pitch on the accentuated syllable, usually upwards. Say the following words changing to a higher pitch on the syllable to be accentuated:

succeed, imply, detest, tinkle, thimble, water, umbrella, attention, improving, windowsill, syllable, telephone, understand, magazine, afternoon, remarkable, photography, educated, aristocracy, characteristically, identification, industrialization.

Did you notice that as the number of syllables increased there was a natural tendency to introduce more than one pitch lift? The highest pitched syllable is termed the **primary accentuation**, lower peaks used are called **secondary accentuations**. Thus we can have a pitch pattern for a word when it is said in isolation. However, within a sentence the pitch pattern on syllables varies according to the sense and construction for the phrases involved. We'll be discussing that later on.

Before leaving change of pitch and accentuation, try saying the following words changing to a lower pitch on the accentuated syllable or syllables:

detest, revolt, disgusting, inevitable, evil, concerned, doldrums, rubbish, ghastly, failure, umbrage, irascibility, grumpy, maliciousness.

Did you create any type of atmosphere by lowering the pitch instead of raising it? Investigate the following words with regard to accentuation:

absent, conduct, contract, digest, envelope, export, object, perfect, perfume, present, produce, progress, rebel, record, refuse, subject, minute.

Emphasis is the creation of the importance of a word in a phrase by the use of vocal and visual techniques. One of the techniques that may be used is a change of pitch, either a change to a higher or a lower note on the word to be emphasised. With mono-syllabic words, the whole word is placed on the different pitch; with multi-syllabic words there is the increase in pitch change on the accentuated syllable. Take the sentence:

I'm going to the circus tomorrow night.

Listen to the effect on the ear as each of the following syllables is lifted in turn. Aim to keep the syllables not lifted on a level middle pitch: *I'm, go . . ., cir . . .,. .mor. . . , night.* That was a mechanical exercise. Now repeat it introducing the following thoughts as you say the sentence:

I'm	– boasting that your friend is not going to the cinema.
go . . .	– no one is going to stop me.
cir . .	– excitedly, I'm not going to the circus.
mor .	– not tonight.
night	– not for the afternoon performance.

Now say the sentence naturally as a statement. Did you hear the two natural peaks on *cir . . .* and *night?* There were also slight pressures on *go . . .* and *. . mor . . .* This regularity of alternation of pressure and pitch change contributes much to the **rhythm of delivery**.

Practise the following sentences, extracting as many different meanings as possible by changing the pitch on the syllables in order. Of course it would not make sense to lift pitch in minor words such as *of, for, as, to, on,* except in special circumstances:

Will you do this for me?
That is the best of the three-roomed flats.
Sheila Wright was the first to arrive at the meeting.
Where are the blueprints John drew up last August?

Finally, say aloud the following conversation observing the natural pitch changes to point the changing emphasis. If you can practise this with a partner, so much the better.

A: *Thelma has arrived.*
B: *Thelma Green?*
A: *Thelma White.*
B: *Not the Thelma White?*
A: *Thelma White the writer.*
B: *Thelma White the writer from Yorkshire?*
A: *Lancashire.*
B: *I could have sworn it was Yorkshire.*
A: *No, Lancashire.*
B: *Oh, yes, she was born in Yorkshire, then she went to live in Lancashire.*
A: *Her father kept a grocer's shop.*
B: *Her mother kept the grocer's shop.*
A: *Then her father must have had the green grocer's in Vicarage Road.*
B: *The green grocer's in Priory Walk.*
A: *Let's go and meet her.*
B: *You can, I can't stand the sight of her.*

Change of Thought

At times it is necessary, and also effective, to change the pitch to introduce a change of thought or mood. A change to a lower pitch is required to introduce a parenthesis. A change to a higher pitch is used to introduce a new bright topic, whereas a lower pitch would be used to introduce a more serious topic. Apply these broad rules as you say the following paragraph aloud:

"Tommy Wiseman, who had just arrived home from his American tour, began to relate his experiences. He started in San Francisco, the city with the famous Golden Gate bridge, and recalled the fast

tempo of life there. His arrival in Washington D.C. coincided with the huge and exciting presidential election campaign. Finally, there was a depressing visit to the poorer outskirts of Chicago, the notorious gangster city of the past."

With a double parenthesis there is the initial lowering of pitch to start the first parenthesis and then a slight raising of note to introduce the second. As with all parentheses there is a resumption of the previous pitch used before the parenthesis was started. A broad pattern of the shape of the double parenthesis could be like this:

Jean Gaunt   *collapsed*
                    who is currently in the West End
          the leading actress

Emotional Involvement

There is also the artistic use of pitch which is mainly associated with emotional content. Generally speaking, a high pitch would indicate high spirits such as excitement, joy, anticipation; but could also be used for hysterical anger. The low pitch range suggests low spirits such as dejection, sorrow, weariness, tiredness; as well as mystery, secrecy, fear, and contained anger. Middle pitch is used for ordinary conversation and narration where there is no emotional involvement.

Take the following sentences and say them aloud using a pitch appropriate to each of the emotions indicated after each:

"It's a scandal". (secrecy, with hilarity, disgustedly).
"Oh, to see the event first hand". (dread, excitedly, mysteriously).
"Just wait one moment". (with contained anger, happily).

To conclude this section on pitch, consider the choice of pitch and characterisation. What overall pitch could you use when depicting the following characters: *a stage butler, a nervous spinster, a military type, a very masculine type of woman, a fop?*

75 Remember when portraying two characters, or when reading a selection containing narrative and characters, appropriate pitch changes must be used to indicate the change of speakers and their change of thoughts and moods.

76 PACE. This is the variation of, or balance between, the rates used in delivery. Rate can be fast, medium or slow, plus gradations in between. A bad pace means that an even rate has been adopted when speaking; this even rate may be too fast or too slow, the former produces a gabble, the latter results in a plodding monotony. Good pace is achieved by varying the rate of delivery.

Techniques of Pace

77   There are several technical rules for the choice of rate.

(a) As a change from accentuation by variation of pitch on a syllable, one can produce the accent by increasing the duration when uttering the syllable. This is achieved mainly by dwelling on the vowels and certain sustained consonants. Determine the syllable to be accentuated in the following words and, without altering pitch, stretch the duration of the syllable chosen:

aghast, alone, beseech, weary, sweeping, homeward, sarcastic, referee, plausible, unfortunate.

You should have noticed that increasing the duration of a syllable is easier if the syllable contains a long monophthong or a compound vowel.

(b) To emphasise a whole word or phrase and give it prominence a slowing down of rate would be used; whereas there would be a speeding up on unimportant words and phrases, including a parenthesis. Practise the following sentence, shifting the importance by slowing down on different parts of the sentence — keep the rate even on the rest:

The chances of fleeing the country are remote.

Stretch	*chances*	to mean the extreme gamble.
	fleeing	to mean we could stay here easily.
	count . .	to mean we could get out of the town.
	. . mote	to mean definitely not easy.

Now do the same with the following sentences and in each case state aloud the intention behind the slowing down of the rate:

The child was not wholly to blame.
The rule is plain, gambling is not allowed.
So, it was you I saw in the wood.
It was a cool day, I remember too well.

A slowing down of the rate would also be made on unfamiliar words such as place names, people's names, chemicals, new processes or products and so on. This is in fact, another example of emphasis.

(c) One important determination of the choice of rate is your capability of neat and accurate articulation. With difficult consonantal combinations, the rate has to be adjusted to ensure a clear formation of all the speech sounds. Revise here the tongue twisters given in chapter five.

(d) When choosing our appropriate rate for delivery the size and acoustics of the room must be considered. A slower overall rate is needed in a large room with an echo than in a smaller, intimate room where contact with the audience is more speedily attained.

(e) The type of audience should also be ascertained. Some audiences composed of the elderly, the slightly deaf, the mentally retarded and also those whose native language is not English cannot comprehend as quickly as people without some deficiency, hence a slower rate must be adopted.

(f) Finally, increasing the duration of the major syllables, and compensating for this by a quickening of the subordinate words and phrases can help to produce an insistent rhythm. Build up the following series of sentences stretching the words *Charles, Scotland, Wednesday, Bertha, Jamaica* and *Thursday* and lightly skipping over the other words with just a slight extra beat or a change of pitch on the syllables — *told, -fore, -range-, -cuss-, trav-, -rives, sis-, com-, joins.* Experiment with this suggestion as an exercise, but remember there are several variations to the rhythmical patterns which can be created. Now for the sentences:

1. *Charles arrives on Wednesday.*
2. *Charles arrives on Wednesday and Bertha joins us on Thursday.*
3. *Charles, who will be travelling from Scotland, arrives on Wednesday and Bertha joins us on Thursday.*
4. *Charles, who will be travelling from Scotland, arrives on Wednesday and Bertha, who is coming from Jamaica, joins us on Thursday.*
5. *Charles, who will be travelling from Scotland, arrives on Wednesday and Bertha, his sister-in-law, who is coming from Jamaica, joins us on Thursday.*
6. *As I told you before, Charles who will be travelling from Scotland arrives on Wednesday and Bertha, his sister-in-law, who is coming from Jamaica, joins us on Thursday.*

7. *As I told you before when the arrangements were discussed,*
   Charles, who will be travelling from Scotland, arrives on
   Wednesday and Bertha, his sister-in-law, who is coming from
   Jamaica, joins us on Thursday.

Can you hear the rhythm? Possibly you could go on to amplify this
sentence even more, giving details of places and times of arrival and
departure, but such a sentence would be very cumbersome.

By now you should begin to realise that mechanical rules are only
a guide line, and that the interpretation of a piece of writing is
determined by the mind with regard to sense and imagination; but
there is still the emotional aspect to consider which can colour and
bend or break the rules. Naturalness and spontaneity must also be
present to avoid a stilted effect.

Emotional Aspects of Pace

78 Artistically, the choice of rate, as in the case of pitch, is
bound up to some extent with emotion. An excited state of mind or
an elated mood is reflected in a quicker rate of delivery. A more
serious or dejected frame of mind demands a slower delivery. From
aesthetic considerations of the meanings of words and the images
they create, one might linger awhile or speed up on the delivery of
certain words. Even the sound qualities chosen in the words can
direct your imagination to say *dwell here* or *sweep over there* with a
maximum effect.

Read the following aloud, varying the rate to heighten the value
or effect of words, but take care you do not overdo it or the result
will be a contrived box of tricks full of vocal embellishments:

The ploughman homeward plods his weary way.

The sea is calm tonight.

Wrap thy form in a mantle gray,
   Star – in wrought!
Blind with thine hair the eyes of Day;
Kiss her until she be wearied out,
Then wander o'er city, and sea, and land,
Touching all with thine opiate wand –
   Come, long – sought!

Merrily, merrily shall I live now
Under the blossom that hangs on the bough.

And this is why I sojourn here,
Alone and palely loitering,
Though the sedge is wither'd from the lake,
And no birds sing.

I am sneered at by all my acquaintance, and paragraphed in the
newspapers.

Where the quick dipper forages
In elver-peopled crevices.

Finally, one can use a slow rate to indicate a reflective mood or a struggle to recall the past. If this is followed by a quick rate, the effect of spontaneity can be achieved as the latter ideas seem to pour out of the memory.

79 POWER. This is the degree of force, loudness or volume placed on a syllable, word or phrase. When considering a word, the term stress is used. As with the cases of the use of pitch and rate, power can be used for accentuation of syllables, for the emphasis of words and the creation of rhythm. These three elements of expression are intricately used in an infinite variety of ways to produce an abundance of speech patterns, aiding the sense and artistic interpretation.

Repeat the exercises given for pitch and pace, relying this time on increase of power to accentuate and emphasise. Next, repeat the work given earlier in connection with the change of thought (page 98). Can you hear that by relying only on power to emphasise, a very military and sometimes jerky effect is produced? Obviously there must be a judicious use of the facets of vocal expression to produce an aesthetically satisfying result.

Vocal Climax

80 Gradual increase of power, together with a stepping up in pitch on successive phrases can help to create climax. Appreciate this as you read part of a famous speech, given by Brutus in *Julius Caesar:*

"As Caesar loved me, I weep for him; as he was fortunate, I rejoice at it; as he was valiant, I honour him; but as he was ambitious, I slew him".

81 Try the following exercises with a view to increasing your awareness of the value of power (often called tone quantity):

a Sing the long monophthongs with increasing then diminishing power.

b Pulsate on the nasal consonants *m, n* and *ng.*

c Choose the power or force appropriate when the following sentences are spoken, think also about what pitch and rate are used:

I'm too excited to speak.
It was an ordinary day which produced ordinary events.
Curse you! It's all your fault! Why can't you be reasonable.
Little by little, the force of the spoken word becomes increasingly powerful until it conquers in the end.
Listen, and keep very still, there's someone creeping about outside.

82 PAUSE. This is technically a cessation of speech, but under certain artistic conditions may be merely a suspension of the word flow. In other words, a pause may be complete where there is a silence or it may be partial where the speaker dwells on a syllable. To illustrate these two types of pause, let's have a look first of all at the sense pauses.

Sense Pauses

83 In chapter one we said that phrasing is the grouping of words into ideas, each phrase creating a certain image. When speaking, think of phrases as thought packets which one delivers to the audience on a series of vocal impulses, according to the number of syllables in the phrase, after which there is a pause to allow the audience time to absorb what has been spoken. Sense pauses do coincide with the punctuation. Punctuation, however, is a graphical device designed to guide the eye. Phrasing appeals to the ear.

Consider this sentence: *The old lady and the young boy walked up the hill. When they got to the top, they lit a fire. The weather was fine and they had a lovely picnic.*

Here we have seven mental pictures — seven phrases. We have pictures of an old lady, a young boy, walking up a hill, reaching the top, lighting a fire, a fine day and an enjoyable picnic. The first three images are linked, so a slight dwelling could be made on *lady* and *boy* — these would be partial pauses. After *hill* a complete pause could be made and if necessary a breath taken. Another partial pause could be made on the word *top* followed by a complete pause after *fire*. Lastly, one more partial pause on the word *fine,* and a terminal, complete pause obviously after *picnic.* No breath should be taken on partial pauses. To represent this in writing below, a partial pause is indicated by an asterisk * and a complete pause by a stroke. So one interpretation of the use of sense pauses could be:

*The old lady * and the young boy * walked up the hill. / When they got to the top * they lit a fire. / The weather was fine * and they had a lovely picnic. /*

Determine the phrasing in the following paragraph:

TRAVELS WITH A DONKEY IN THE CEVENNES

Night is a dead monotonous period under a roof; but in the open world it passes lightly, with its stars and dews and perfumes, and the hours are marked by changes in the face of Nature. What seems a kind of temporal death to people choked between walls and curtains, is only a light and living slumber to the man who sleeps afield. All night long he can hear Nature breathing deeply and freely; even as she takes her rest she turns and smiles; and there is one stirring hour unknown to those who dwell in houses, when a wakeful influence goes abroad over the sleeping hemisphere, and all the outdoor world are on their feet. It is then that the cock first crows, not this time to announce the dawn, but like a cheerful watchman speeding the course of night. Cattle awake on the meadows; sheep break their fast on dewy hillsides, and change to a new lair among the ferns; and houseless men, who have lain down with their fowls, open their dim eyes and behold the beauty of the night.

Robert Louis Stevenson

Dramatic Pauses

84 In addition to the sense pauses there are pauses for effect, often called dramatic pauses. There are at least three different dramatic pauses.

1 The rhetorical pause. This is a pause placed before a word to make the audience ask a mental question about, or to anticipate what is to follow:

What we must do is to / destroy him.
Could we possibly / start again?

2 **The oratorical pause.** This is a pause placed after a word to make the audience reflect upon what has been said:

What we need are guns / not men* to win this war.
He is a millionaire / you know.

Of course, for extreme dramatic effect, a pause can be made both before and after the emphatic word:

The verdict is / death / a unanimous verdict.

3 **The emotional pause.** In order to indicate a disturbed state of mind due to extreme sorrow, anger or tiredness, the emotional pause can be used. This is an illogical pause, placed anywhere in the sentence, to indicate the confused mental state:

I am / so / angry I can hardly / speak.
The whole / experience has so / shattered me I could / sleep for / a week.

85 PAUSES ASSOCIATED WITH VERSE

Verse pause. Obvious one and needs no elaboration since it is a pause used to separate verses when the sense does not flow on.

Suspensory or suspensive pause. This is similar to the partial pause mentioned earlier. It occurs at the end of an enjambed or unstopped line of verse, that is at the end of a line of verse, where the sense flows on to the next line. The method of handling this is to linger on the final word of the unstopped line. In reality, it is a suspension of rate and pitch, giving the effect of a pause. One could say that often an upward vocal glide takes place on the final word, before the delivery sweeps on to the next line. No breath is taken in at this pause. Examples:

Hear it not Duncan, it is a knell
That summons thee to heaven or to hell

I wandered lonely as a cloud
That floats on high o'er vales and hills

When I consider how my light is spent
Ere half my days, in this dark world and wide,

And when I pressed the shell
Close to my ear
And listened well,
And straightway like a bell
Came low and clear
The slow, sad murmur of the distant seas,
Whipped by an icy breeze
Upon a shore
Wind-swept and desolate.

Metrical Pause

Sometimes, as with the case of the above extracts, the lines of the verse are of irregular length, and yet there is some rhyming scheme. To keep the overall shape of the poem, **metrical pauses** are used. These usually are of the partial type and serve, in fact, to stretch certain words in the shorter lines so that the overall duration for each line becomes approximately the same. In some poems, metrical feet are missing and so the metrical pause is used to compensate:

Break, / Break, / Break,
On the cold grey stones O Sea!

The caesural pause is literally a cutting or a pause placed at some points other than the end of the line of verse. It usually occurs after the main emphatic word in the line. No breath need be taken at this pause:

The quality of mercy / is not strain'd;
It droppeth, / as the gentle rain from heaven
Upon the place beneath: / it is twice bless'd
It blesseth him that give / and him that takes:
'Tis mightiest in the mightiest; / it becomes
The throned monarch / better than his crown.

86 INFLECTION. When we were discussing pitch, we said that a small leap up or down in pitch is used to establish accentuation and also emphasis. If instead of a leap in the change of pitch, a glide from one note to another is made, this is called an inflection. So we can define inflection as the sliding of the voice from one note to another. It is this sliding of the voice which distinguishes speech from singing. When singing, one changes note without a slide; when speaking one is continually making gentle glides from note to note.

The overall pattern of changes of pitch, coupled with inflections is called **intonation**. There are several different types of inflection. These are as follows:

Simple inflections. These are glides either upwards or downwards and hence are called simple rising inflection or simple falling inflection. These inflections are often heard when answering the telephone, eg. *(Hello)* *"Yes?"* *(Is that you Mary?)* *"Yes"* *(confirmed).*

Double or circumflex inflections. Here we have two glides in the voice, either down-up or up-down. The inflection is named according to its final turn. So these inflections are double rising and double falling. If double inflections are used, there is an extra meaning implied other than an affirmative (yes) or negative (no). For instance if you are asked a question and your reply is a doubtful "yes" a double rising inflection would most probably be used. *"Will you be at the meeting tonight?"* *"Yes".* With a shocked surprise, answer to that question as if to imply "why on earth should you ask", the tune would be a compound falling inflection *"Yes".*

With more extreme emotions and deeper implications, three slides or glides of the voice may be used. This type of inflection is termed compound eg. *"Have you heard about Jane?"* *"Yes"* (and I know more about it than you do!) or *"Yes"* (I should like you to tell me and then I'll give you my version of the incident).

Of course, one has to use the ear to appreciate all the nuances and implications that can be achieved by the use of inflection. Intensity of inflection is the degree of slide and this reflects the emotional intensity of the speaker. Try these exercises aloud, increasing the amount of slide as the intensity of emotion increases:

"Is that you, Jack?" *"Yes"* (matter of fact)
"Are you sure?" *"Yes"* (emphatically)
"Do you really intend to invest in the scheme?" *"Yes"* (I've said so many times)
"You're sure you are wise?" *"Yes"* (for the final time, slamming down the phone).

Summing up, we can say that simple inflections are used for simple ideas and double and compound inflections are used when extra emotions are to be conveyed, such as sarcasm, irony, doubt, surprise, etc.

The Law of Suspense and Conclusion

87 The main use of inflection is to indicate the sense rather than produce variety in delivery. If we were to use rising and falling cadences repetitively, the effect would be a mere artificial vocal undulation and the meaning would be lost. There are, however, some broad guide lines concerning the use of inflection. The most basic rule is termed "the law of suspense and conclusion", which states that **"when the sense is incomplete (or doubtful) or if you wish to keep your hearers in suspense an upward inflection is made at the end of the phrase. When the sense is complete a downward slide is used."** However, in continuous speech one rarely uses only simple inflections to indicate incompleteness or completeness, the effect would be very mechanical. Even if no extra implications were intended, it is more artistic to use double inflections rather than simple ones. Use a double rising inflection when the sense is incomplete and a double falling to indicate completeness. Take care, however, that these inflections are gentle ones or the effect would be a vocal switch-back. The same technique can be used at the end of an unstopped line of verse, the gentle fall before the rise indicates artistically that the sense flows on to the next line.

88 There are certain rules for the use of inflection of statements, questions, imperatives and exclamations. These rules are only rough guides and must be respected with integrity. Avoid becoming a slave to rules or your speech will be stilted, unimaginative, inartistic and lacking spontaneity. Let us deal first of all with statements.

Inflection of a Statement

Statements can be simple, co-ordinate or complex sentences. Here the law of suspense and conclusion will generally apply, however, note these examples concerning lists of things, or series as they are called technically. **A concluding series** is a list after the verb. If there is no dramatic ingredient in the list, an upward inflection is made on each member of the series, except the last one which takes a downward slide:

On the way home I passed Hyde Park, Green Park and Kensington Gardens.

However, if the list has dramatic qualities, the following becomes the tune:

We must have guns, ammunition and men.

The downward inflections produce emphasis. Sometimes the list of articles precedes the verb, this series is called a **commencing series** as distinct from the previous series called concluding. If the commencing series is unemphatic, a rising inflection is made on each member except the penultimate one, on which there is a falling slide:

Apples, oranges, pears and bananas were all lying scattered around.

With dramatic intensity, each member of the commencing series takes a downward inflection:

Death, disease, destruction and torture, all were present all the time.

Inflections can be used to point contrasts or **antitheses**. If two things are contrasted, we call that single antithesis, with two pairs of objects we have double antithesis, and when three pairs are contrasted it is called triple antithesis. The speech tunes used are as follows:

single: *The day was fine not rainy*

double: *The king was in the counting house, the queen was in the parlour.*

triple: *In winter we have hot chocolate, in summer we have iced coffee.*

Inflection of a Question

Questions can be **real** or **pseudo**. A real question is one to which the speaker does not know the answer and genuinely wants a reply. A pseudo question is one which is asked when the speaker does not want a reply, or thinks he knows the answer, or it's a question containing emotion of some kind. Let us start with real questions. These may be of two kinds, those requiring an answer "yes" or "no", and those requiring a statement answer. The first kind takes an upward inflection, the second requires a downward inflection as indicated in the following sentences for practice:

real questions requiring an answer	
'yes' or 'no'	**full statement**
Are you going out?	*Where are you going?*
Is this your first visit?	*Which way is the garden?*

The pie is ready?   *What did you do yesterday?*

Will you be going to-day?   *When does the postman deliver?*

The book is found?

With pseudo questions the rule is reversed:

Is this a dagger I see before me?

Will you please be quiet?

Where did you say he went?   (a repeated question)

How can you do this to me?   (pleading emotion)

Inflection of Commands or Entreaties

Both are, in fact, imperatives. The former take a downward inflection, the latter an upward one. Practise the following aloud:

as a command	*Get out of my sight.*
as an order	*Give me some bread.*
begging for it	*Give me some bread.*
politely	*Come in.*
bad-temperedly	*Come in.*

Exclamations   take a downward inflection:

Help!   *Confound it!*   *Zounds!*

Although so much can be conveyed by the use of subtle inflection, there is much more comic effect which can also be created by using extreme intensities. Practise the following aloud: *Oh! Yes. Mm..Well,* using appropriate inflections to convey the moods as listed below:

archly	*icily*	*querrulously*
blithely	*jokingly*	*robustly*
cautiously	*kindly*	*slyly*
definitely	*languidly*	*triumphantly*
excitedly	*murderously*	*understandingly*
forlornly	*nostalgically*	*vehemently*
grudgingly	*offensively*	*winsomely*
haughtily	*painfully*	*youthfully*
		zealously

89 There you have an almost complete alphabetical list of various adverbs indicating the moods. Of course, you can expand this list many times, and it will be a very good exercise to promote vocal expression and flexibility. Take such adverbs and practise saying phrases and sentences of your own choice, trying to convey vocally the particular sentiment behind them. Besides being a useful exercise in inflection work, such practice also introduces tones which is the final section of this chapter.

90 TONE. As mentioned earlier in chapter four, tone is a good vocal quality or timbre. Let us concentrate on tone colouring, which is the adjustment of the tonal quality to convey emotion. This has to be done mentally, and no amount of writing here concerning the change in the shape of the resonators will yield results. If you believe and are sincere in your emotion, it will be transmitted through your voice as **tone colour**, providing there are no organic defects. The alphabetical exercise given in the previous paragraph will help here. Use also such phrases as *I can't help it; Give it to me* and *Will you do it?* expressing contrasts in tonal colouring, eg. warmth or coldness, smoothness or roughness, harshness or gentleness, tension or relaxation. There is no limit to the number of exercises you can devise for yourself in order to improve your vocal expression. Here are some, which can prove both profitable and pleasurable. Work, if possible, with a partner, and try to interpret the following short duologues in at least three different ways each, paying attention to vocal contrasts and variation of character and choice of situation.

Exercise 1 In the course of the duologue, try to shift the dominance of *b* to *a*, leaving *b* at the end thoroughly miserable:

a. *Are you all right?*
b. *Yes.*
a. *Are you sure?*
b. *Certainly.*
a. *You don't look well.*
b. *I'm perfectly well.*
a. *Had a bad night?*
b. *I had a good night.*

a. *Are you off your food?*
b. *I'm enjoying my food.*
a. *Perhaps it's your job.*
b. *My job's fine.*
a. *It could be 'flu.*
b. *I had that last month.*
a. *Or the weather.*
b. *I like this weather.*
a. *It upsets some people.*
b. *It suits me.*
a. *You look after yourself.*
b. *Thanks. I will.*

Exercise 2 An interesting example of shifting emphasis. Introduce such moods as exasperation, provocation, hilarity, ridicule and so on.

a. *Albert's growing up quickly, isn't he?*
b. *Albert? Surely you mean Arthur?*
a. *Arthur, Anthony, Alistair and Albert isn't it?*
b. *In that order.*
a. *Arthur is ten next birthday.*
b. *He is eleven next birthday.*
a. *He was born the same year that Lily married.*
b. *He was five the year father died.*
a. *That makes him ten.*
b. *Father died six years ago.*
a. *Father died five years ago.*
b. *Father died the same year that we bought this house.*
a. *How time flies!*

Now just experiment with the remaining exercises that appear on page 114.

Exercise 3

a. *Some people!*
b. *I know.*
a. *Did you see that?*
b. *Yes.*
a. *People are so rude.*
b. *Very rude!*
a. *They don't care.*
b. *They're ignorant.*
a. *They've no manners.*
b. *I blame the parents.*
a. *Parents haven't a clue.*
b. *And, of course, schools.*
a. *What do they learn there?*
b. *They just play.*
a. *A sheer waste of taxes.*

Exercise 4

a. *Don't move.*
b. *Why not?*
a. *There's a beetle.*
b. *Where?*
a. *On your neck.*
b. *Get it off.*
a. *Oh! It's moved.*
b. *Oh!*
a. *No. No.*
b. *No what?*
a. *It isn't a beetle.*
b. *What is it?*
a. *I don't know.*

Exercise 5

a. *Fetch him.*
b. *But he's ill.*
a. *Fetch him.*
b. *But he'll die.*
a. *Yes. He'll die.*
b. *You couldn't.*
a. *Couldn't I?*
b. *He's so old.*
a. *Yes. Too old.*
b. *You're evil.*
a. *Am I?*
b. *Be kind.*
a. *What for?*
b. *For my sake.*
a. *For your sake?*

Exercise 6

a. *You're a puppet.*
b. *I can do what I like.*
a. *He owns you.*
b. *And go where I wish.*
a. *You'd lick his boots.*
b. *I admire his gifts.*
a. *You follow him around.*
b. *I like his voice.*
a. *Even when he shouts?*
b. *That's just his way.*
a. *He's so rude.*
b. *That's what I like.*
a. *What, rude people?*
b. *No, people with character.*
a. *Is that what he has?*

CHAPTER TEN

SPEAKING TO OTHERS

91 Scientifically, communication demands a transmitter, a message and a receiver. However, it matters not how strong the signals are which are sent out from the television station, and how erudite the message is, there will be no reception if the television set is switched off. The same fact must be faced with oral communication. We must have a listener, who is just as important as the speaker. Speaking and listening is a two-way process. This is illustrated in all walks of life, especially in conversation where some comment is made and is immediately picked up by the attentive listener who then adds to the general repartee with comments of his own. There follows a ping-pong state with both primary speaker and primary listener contributing as much as each other to the overall communication.

This chapter will deal with the formal methods of making such communications as introducing a speaker, giving a vote of thanks, structuring the informative and persuasive speeches, and some tips on interviews. First, however, we must discuss the attitude towards speaking in public, whether it be to one person, a hundred, a thousand or by ways of mass media to millions. The basic attitude should be the same for each. Let us therefore consider, first of all, what points to cultivate and what to avoid as speakers.

GENERAL CONSIDERATIONS FOR SPEAKERS

1 Preliminary Training
Obviously, the technical side of communication has to be mastered. This involves exercises in relaxation, breathing, voice production. sound formation and expression. Any tendency towards tension, bad breath control, inaccurate speech or dull presentation must be carefully cured. Exercises given throughout this book would amply cover these important points.

A lucid and appropriate vocabulary must be attained and practised, until ease is acquired in its use in connected speech. Make the choice of vocabulary suitable both for content and audience. Don't talk above your audience's intelligence.

Think of speaking as giving pleasure or benefit to others. You are imparting information which could be of help to your audience: Sound enthusiastic as if you wish to share an experience with others. Avoid thinking that you are unworthy to speak, or that you have nothing to say. Why should you have been invited to speak unless your topic and yourself are desired?

2   Approach to the Talk

Long before you make your appearance, devote as much time as possible to preparation. Read up your subject, even if you think you know it very well, there are always some points you tend to omit. Research around the subject as well, so that you are prepared for all manner of questions that may arise.

Pay attention to appearance. Be neat and well groomed rather than striving to impress with the latest "gear" or ultra-sophisticated Paris model. Jewelry can distract. Conspicuous baubles, bangles and beads draw the attention of the listeners away from the content of your talk to their sight and sound.

Allow yourself plenty of time to journey to the meeting or interview. Always arrive early so that you can compose yourself and take stock of the acoustics of the hall. It also gives you time to have that confidential chat with the organiser or secretary. It's surprising what useful little tips arise from such an informal conversation about the attitude of the audience, eg. who is hard of hearing, who is the "expert", what the interviewer is like, what mood is he in, etc.

3   Contact with the Audience

Make eye contact to ensure rapport/and friendliness, but do not stare into the eyes of a listener. It can be embarrassing if you focus your attention on the listener's face or on one particular member of your audience. Let your eyes make contact with as many people as possible, but avoid making it mechanical, otherwise the effect could resemble a Wimbledon head movement from side to side.

Whilst on the matter of eye focus and contact, do avoid talking over the heads (physically) of your audience, and also avoid talking at so many bodies. Make your contact with the audience continuous, and avoid restless gazing around at the ceiling or floor, or even out of the window. Open the eyes when communicating, it is most disconcerting to be confronted by a speaker with half-closed eyes. Such a speaker seems bored and lacking alertness. Try to adopt a pleasant facial approach, with a smile where appropriate. Avoid the fixed, artificial grin betraying insincerity and indifference.

Above all — be humane to your audience. Be concerned for their comfort. Can they see you? Can they hear you without an apparent effort? Try to create the atmosphere that you are talking to individuals. As you deliver your talk, retain that friendly sincerity and be authoritative without being pompous or condescending. Cultivate the use of an occasional pause, whilst you consciously take a breath through the nose. This will also help you to relax, should some nervous tension creep in, and reduce the tendency to introduce the "gap fillers" such as *er, um, now then, right now, you know,* etc.

4 Coping with 'Butterflies'

Everyone has nerves or butterflies to some degree. Actually, it is not an entirely detrimental phenomenon; slight nerves can prompt inspiration and bring about a certain magic of the performance. However, uncontrolled nerves are a menace and can result in a muddled, hesitant delivery or, in an extreme case, a total break down.

Therefore, just before you start, tense your body and then completely flop, preferably several times. This will help relaxation. Also take some deep breaths to steady your nerves.

Mention has been made in chapter two of the statement *"apply reason to your fear".* It is so important that a reiteration is in order here. Almost always, the audience is on your side, so is the interviewer or examiner. If you are well prepared, you will gain confidence to present your facts from knowing that you will not meet any animosity in your audience.

GENERAL CONSIDERATIONS FOR LISTENERS

1 Attention

Generally give out to your speaker by showing him that you are genuinely interested in his topic, and that you want to listen. Avoid listening with closed eyes, it is most off-putting to a speaker. Open the eyes to show alertness. Use the head, brows and lips to indicate that you are responding to the talk. However, don't do this forcibly or mechanically lest the result becomes one of insincerity.

During interviews and conversation avoid putting up barriers such as slumping back in your seat, head in hand, elbow on chair etc. Another barrier is to sit with arms folded, legs crossed, lips squeezed or putting on a frown. These attitudes also create the 'go on, convince me' atmosphere. The same detrimental atmosphere could be introduced by the hand covering the lower part of the listener's face, so that only a pair of disbelieving eyes are revealed.

Adopt a slightly forward-leaning posture. It produces a friendly eagerness to listen and learn. When having a conversation, punctuate occasionally with sincere comments such as *'I agree', 'That's new', 'That's interesting', 'Really?', 'You're right',* etc. This however, needs careful application or it will sound false.

Avoid simulated listening while doing something else such as writing and addressing envelopes, making diary entries, reading notes, etc. No amount of 'You carry on, I'm listening, don't let it disturb you . . . etc' will help. The speaker would invariably acquire a sense of failure in drawing the undivided attention of the listeners. Doodling is another bad habit of a listener. If you are prone to doodling, put away all scrap paper and discipline yourself to completing the interview form, if one is used. Also avoid fidgeting with your hands or objects such as keys or a handkerchief.

2 Concentration

Don't keep letting your attention wander by looking out of the window, or studying your programme, or glancing at the clock too often. Try not to get distracted by extraneous noise and movements such as the passing of a low-flying aircraft, or the howling of the ambulance and, of course, the arrival of latecomers.

In conversation, or even in interviews, make sure you understand what the speaker is saying. If you have reasonable doubts, ask pertinent questions. Don't question with your face, the bewildered or puzzled frown does not aid communication. Smile and apologise for interrupting, then firmly but politely ask a positive question. Don't add detrimental comments such as *'I'm afraid you aren't being very explicit'* or *'That's not good enough for me'* etc. Those are negative remarks and hardly could promote improvement in communication. It is far more conducive to good two-way speaking to ask instead *'That's most interesting. Would you refresh my memory over your proposal just once more, please? I want to make it absolutely clear in my mind'.*

3   Question Time

It is a compliment to any speaker if you review the main points of the conversation or interview, occasionally. Obviously, you cannot do this in a public gathering. A good speaker will stimulate his audience to think. As a good listener, allow yourself to have an open mind and ask mental questions as the talk proceeds. Any questions unanswered by the speaker in the course of his address may be put to him at the end of the session.

A word now about questions. Formulate your questions in simple, straightforward language. Keep them brief and to the point. Use one question for one subject. The multi-subject question is confusing in the extreme, both for the speaker and for the rest of the audience. Avoid airing your own views in question time, it's the speaker's views you are interested in. Beware of trying to sound the authority, much more is to be gained by an air of humility. Cultivate a friendly tone when posing your questions.

93 Many people find it difficult to ask questions succinctly. You can practise at home in this way. Listen to the news headlines on the radio and ask three pertinent questions aloud. Listen to a short talk on the television or radio, and again ask no more than three questions on the subject matter at the end. You may say that you forgot your questions by the end of the talk. Adopt the practice of choosing key words to jog your memory. For instance should the talk have been on rehousing problems, you may wish to ask questions on social amenities, the problems of how to get to and from the estate to the present place of work, and finally rent control. As the talk proceeds, bend a finger for each topic you query, and associate a finger with a key word. In the above example, key words could be *entertainment, travel, rent.* As each topic is discussed, release one of the fingers.

94 CONVERSATION. Remember   that   conversation   is essentially a two-way process, each participant has to offer and has

to receive. It is a bad conversation if one person is too dominant and monopolises the situation. Conversation is a sharing of experiences and ideas, it is the exchange of views, the justification of disagreements without a heated slanging match — no one ever won an argument.

In conversation one has to be flexible, allowing oneself to appreciate the other person's views without deprecation or forcing one's own views. Good conversation has information or comment, at the end of which there is a verbal and mental hook on which the listener can latch and further expand the subject.

Avoid abruptly changing the subject, it produces a very jerky effect, and can often be discourteous. You can prepare for conversations by taking stock of your background, your interests, your work, your travels, your hopes, your successes and failures, your home and family, your outlook on current events, your approach to entertainment. You will really be very surprised at the length of the list you can make, if you settle down to it. Try to add to your list in order to widen your topics, and even with existing subjects try to improve your expression of them, consider more vivid vocabulary. Don't try to be the intellectual snob by aiming to use archaic or verbose language. Avoid sprinkling the conversation with academic phrases and foreign expressions. It may be fashionable to use expressions such as *ambiance, genre, a la mode, alter ego, billet doux, bon-viveur* and all the other myriad phrases offered by pseudo-intellectuals, often incorrectly. I once met someone who described a person's form as being a *corpus delicti*.

Starting a Conversation

You can develop conversations, especially with strangers, by asking discrete questions. Don't pry, of course, but the casual question about where they live can lead on to local interests such as sports, fêtes, entertainments, historical monuments, local personalities, etc. From these humble beginnings topics of mutual interest arise, and also points of difference. One can gain information about attitudes to sports, teams watched or not, whether they are viewed in person or on television; this leads on to what else is viewed on the television, what else is applauded or shunned. The avenues are many, but explore one at a time and be prepared for smooth transitions from one subject to another.

Good conversation needs clarity of thought, a suitable rate of exchange of ideas, an attitude of wanting to get to know the other person, a selection of appropriate topics which will stimulate discussion without giving offence or creating barriers, a drawing in of all members of the conversation. Avoid "talking shop" in a company, some will feel left out of matters. Avoid using padding such as this classical example: *"Well, you see, before I make my point I want you to understand, with all the facts under consideration, and bearing in mind any change of public opinion, and frankly I hesitate to commit myself on this point, but I hope you appreciate my position which would, to tell the truth become unbearable with any leakage. But what I mean to say is, if you follow me . . ."* Who could follow that?

Finally, some attitudes to consider. Don't be overbearing or dogmatic. Avoid being argumentative or petulant. Aim to be lively, courteous, sincere and feel that you are offering a contribution to the whole occasion.

95 INTERVIEWS. These are rather more formal conversations but the same attitudes concerning appearance, speech, personality and content apply here. However, quite a lot of preparation can be done before the interview, which will help your confidence and impress the interviewer.

Most rewarding would be research into the following aspects of the organisation concerned: its size, structure, stability, prospects of expansion, policies, products or services offered, executives and connections with local or central government, relationships with other companies or firms, competition from outside sources, and its prestige as well as objectives. From your own point of view, prepare your autobiography, place of birth, parent's histories, your educational background (they always want dates), academic achievements, social interests including sports (find out what emphasis is placed on the social aspects in the company, what clubs are there etc.), and what your ultimate ambition is.

Work out what you could do for the company with regard to your talents and aspirations. Have a rough idea of the salary you expect, otherwise a very direct question *'Well, Mr Jones, what do you think you are worth?'* could prove disconcerting. Do some research into this and don't underestimate your worth nor ridiculously over-price yourself. Payment for an equivalent job in other firms can easily be found out.

Before attending for interviews, work out a series of questions that you may be asked. **Write them down and answer them aloud.**

You might get specific questions such as *"Who gave you the most encouragement in your present career?"* On the other hand, there are those interviewers who give a general opportunity to talk, *"Just carry on and give me all the information about yourself".* Interviewers are prone to setting a "meet-the-situation-problem".

"If you were posted overseas and you couldn't take your family with you, what would be your reaction?" *"There is criticism about one of our products, what investigation would you make to eradicate such criticism?"* *"How would you re-organise the method of dealing with invoices and bad debts in order to reduce the delay of handling?"*

Of course, you may be confronted with more technical questions, but with sound academic training these should not be a problem. If you are more mature and you are attending for an interview, make sure you keep up to date with current methods and ideas. The secret of a successful interview is to be ahead.

96 SOCIAL PUBLIC SPEAKING. This encompasses votes of thanks, introducing speakers, presenting gifts, opening bazaars, toasts and after dinner speeches. For the purposes of this book we shall only deal with the first two topics. Volumes have been written on the more specialised professional techniques required for toasts and after dinner speeches.

Introducing a Speaker

When introducing a speaker, avoid making a mini-speech on your own. Your function is just to stimulate interest in the speaker and his subject, and whet the audience's appetite. You must not over-shadow the speaker in any way. Keep the introduction to a couple of minutes, the audience wants to hear its guest. However, if you perform your duty neatly and effectively without being obtrusive, you most surely will be asked to do the job again.

A mnemonic is an aid to memory. Thus remember the word WAITS. Each letter in this word represents a step in the introduction of a speaker as listed below. You do not have to follow this scheme slavishly, but those of you who are inexperienced may find the formula helpful and confidence building. The main points under each item of the WAITS can be put down on a card. Don't be frightened of using notes, but on the other hand don't become a slave to them. Labouring over one's notes is not conducive to good communication. The delivery also sounds stilted and lacking in spontaneity. The structure is as follows:

W welcome the audience, name the society or function to which the people have arrived, give special welcome to guests and also to the speaker. Don't give his name away yet, there is an element of surprise.

A announce the title of the talk and say that there will be an opportunity to ask questions at the end, which the speaker has kindly agreed to answer (of course, ask the speaker about this beforehand, as he may not wish to tackle questions).

I interest value – opportunity to add a little individual touch here. Say why the audience should be interested in the talk, but don't be vague, be definite. Avoid *'I know, you will be interested in this subject'*, this adds nothing and seems just a feeble bit of padding.

T training and qualifications of the speaker. Do check that this section is accurate and up to date. If at all possible, find out all his credits before the day. It is not very complimentary to approach the speaker just before the talk and ask *'What have you got?'* or *'What have you done?'*. Write out all degrees and diplomas in full. A string of letters such as *'He is a B.A., L.R.A.M., L.L.C.M. (T.D.) and also A.I.S.T.D. (B.B.)* sounds tremendous but is uninformative. Therefore *'He is a bachelor of Arts, a licentiate of the Royal Academy of Music and the London College of Music,* and so on. If you can, introduce any important posts held in his career or any literature written by him, the sense of occasion will be enhanced.

S speaker's name. Be positive here, look at the speaker as you say his name. Don't just say *'I give you so-and-so'* it sounds as if he or she is being thrown to the lions.

Here is a specimen introduction to a speaker visiting a dramatic society:

w *Good evening, ladies and gentlemen, and welcome to the monthly meeting of the Little Watling Dramatic Society. In particular, I should like to welcome those guests our members have brought* *along on this rather bleak winter evening. I hope the warmth of our spirit will be felt by our guests, and possibly they may swell our ranks by considering joining our club. Very special welcome is extended by our committee and members to our distinguished speaker.*

a *Our address this evening is entitled "Characterisation", and our speaker has very kindly agreed to answer any questions you may have at the end of the talk.*

i *Many of you will remember that at the one-act play festival last year, the adjudicator said that although we put up a good show regarding presentation and production, we did fall down somewhat, because of the lack of depth and background to our characterisation. The subject of tonight's talk then should be of great value to all of us.*

t *Our speaker is an Associate of the Drama Board, a member of the Guild of Drama Adjudicators, and has been a tutor in acting at the London Academy of Music and Dramatic Art. He has several books to his credit, his latest being "Timing and Rhythm in Stagecraft". After such an impressive array of qualifications, I know you will be eager to hear tonight's speaker.*

s *Ladies and gentlemen, it gives me very great pleasure to introduce you to Mr. Lincoln Underwood.*

This was quite a formal introduction, but there can still be an air of cordiality in the presentation of it. Sometimes the club members may know the speaker very well, he may even be a member. In this case, a much more fluid introduction may be given. Reference may be made to his contribution to the society's functions and, of course, you can always end up with *"it is always a pleasure to hear from our very dear friend Jack".*

The Vote of Thanks

Again, there is a simple mnemonic to remember, indicating the individual steps in giving a vote of thanks. This one is TRACT, and refers to the following:

T **title contrast,** if you possibly can, try to express the original title of the talk in another befitting way. Suppose the talk had been on *Flower arrangement;* a suitable title contrast would be *How can flowers grace your home.* You see, the person giving the introduction has announced the title, and the speaker has dwelt on the subject. Therefore, it would be more imaginative and artistic to rephrase the title of the talk.

R **relevant point** — select some item of particular relevance from the talk, which stands out in your memory. Make, however, only brief reference to this.

A **addition** — try to add to the relevant point that you have selected from your own experience. Take care though, that you do not make another speech or that you do not destroy what the speaker has established.

C **compliment** the speaker sincerely. Avoid any patronising air, and do not use such phrases as *'I think'* or *'I feel sure';* be positive, say *'I know you will join me in extending a most sincere thank you to our speaker.'*

T **thanks** — add your personal thanks, and look at the speaker when doing so.

Following is an example for a vote of thanks, structured by the above method:

t *Getting into the skin of our parts, obviously, is not as easy as one might think at first sight and our speaker tonight has amply put forward the many various facets of this essential part of acting.*

r *I was particularly interested in the advice Mr. Underwood offered us, concerned with the starting of the creation of our characters from the feet.*

a *This is an excellent comment, and one I can endorse wholeheartedly. I had learnt my lines and moves for a part I was playing, but had not thought much about the shoes I was to wear. On the day of the dress rehearsal, the costumes arrived. I found to my horror that the shoes sent to me completely distorted the walk I was using. Rapidly, I had to rethink the visual aspect of my character and this, in turn, did affect my vocal work. So it is very sound advice "think about your feet".*

c *I know you would want to express your admiration along with mine for the excellent and humorous manner in which Mr. Underwood has tackled the subject this evening. His anecdotes and tips, drawn from his wealth of experience, will long be remembered and will certainly be applied in our forthcoming productions.*

t *And so, it gives me tremendous pleasure to thank you, Mr. Underwood, very much indeed for giving up your very valuable* *time to come here tonight, and give us that informative and entertaining talk. Thank you.*

97 THE INFORMATIVE TALK. This is the most common type of speech that you will have to make. In a minor way, you make one every time you give instructions or information in conversation or on the telephone. Basically, this informative talk is either a **narration, a description** or **an exposition.** The titles listed below will give you examples of each of the three types.

Narration	Cinderella
	A summary of 'Little Women'
	My most frightening experience
Description	My country cottage
	Cubism in art
	The lake district
Exposition	How to travel in Europe on £5 a day
	Starting a collection
	Maintaining your car.

Of course, it must be remembered that these are not water-tight compartments. A talk on this year's holiday might well contain an exposition on how you prepared for the journey, a description of the venue, the hotel, the natives, the other guests, the food, the shopping facilities and so on, and a narration of the day-to-day events. However, the following principles must be observed when giving a strictly informative talk:

1. facts must be presented in a logical manner and must not be concerned with controversial topics,
2. there should be no provocation or argument in the content,
3 the speaker should present the facts without bias.

Having established the principles of the informative talk, the next point to consider is the approach to the audience. The objective here is **to rouse interest, to inform and stimulate curiosity.** As soon as you know you have to give an address, you should complete this exercise — making succinct notes against each item:

general purpose	to inform, narrate or describe
subject	insert your working title (you may modify this later)

specific purpose	this might be an account, a description, a story, an exposition, an outline of a policy or a host of other things. Against this section indicate the gist of your talk.
listeners	try to ascertain how your audience will be composed (age, sex, educational background or experience, occupation, social habits, special interests, prejudices and attitudes)
occasion	indicate why the talk is being given.

Here are a couple of examples showing the practical use of the above method:

A

general purpose	*to inform plus some entertainment*
subject	*experience as a touring actor*
specific purpose	*to give an account of a typical week from the close of the show in one town on a Saturday night to the close of it in another town the next week. Illustrated with amusing anecdotes.*
listeners	*mainly housewives, age range approx. 30 to 65*
occasion	*weekly meeting of the afternoon section of a Townswomen Guild.*

B

general purpose	*to inform*
subject	*I was a Gipsy*
specific purpose	*to describe the life of a roving band of gipsies — the community spirit, hardships, public opinion*
listeners	*mixed audience, mainly professional*
occasion	*monthly meeting of the Round Table.*

Preparation of an Informative Talk

With the above exercises it is assumed that you have been asked to give your address on a specific subject. Very often, the choice is left to you. Choose a topic which is worthy and which will be appropriate for your audience. Limit the scope of the subject according to the time available. One plan to adopt at the preparation stage is to think of a general title and list against it all its sub-divisions. Here is one example of that procedure.

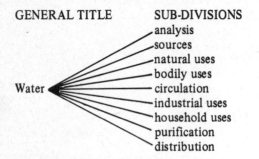

GENERAL TITLE   SUB-DIVISIONS
                       analysis
                       sources
                       natural uses
                       bodily uses
Water   circulation
                       industrial uses
                       household uses
                       purification
                       distribution

Obviously the subject "water" is much too wide to cover in a single lecture. Nine sub-divisions have been created and there are more possibilities. Next you should take a sub-division and further expand that. Let us consider "circulation":

                       in nature
circulation   in plants
                       in animals

Even the extent of this sub-division may be too crowded, since a neat hour's talk could be given on the water cycle in nature only:

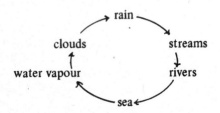

Similarly, the utilisation of water by plants could open up wide possibilities concerning content — osmosis, transportation in xylem, use in photosynthesis, transpiration and so on. In fact, with the more learned, scientifically minded audiences each of these topics could easily be developed into a whole lecture or a series of lectures.

98 Once you have chosen your subject, do some reading about it. Research is invaluable to aid confidence, assurance and authority. Make notes on the points you would like to cover and write each on a separate card. Once you feel that you have enough material, begin to sift out that which is extraneous or distracting. Avoid introducing open-ended facts, they make the audience divert their attention to avenues which are not going to be explored by the speaker. The use of one card — one topic enables you to rearrange the content of your talk until you feel the order is the best one. Check the order for logicality and neat transition from fact to fact.

Structuring of the Informative Talk — INTRODUCTION

As with an essay, a speech must have a beginning, a middle and an end ie. *an introduction, a development and a conclusion.* The introduction serves several purposes. It must engage the audience and stimulate their interest. It allows the audience time to adjust to the speaker's appearance, to his voice and personality. The organisation of the first phase of the talk thus consists of four steps:

1 **the approach**
2 **statement of general aim**
3 **clarification of aim**
4 **preview**

1   In tackling the approach step, engage your listeners by using one of the following opening gambits:

link with the audience — Try to devise some common ground between your audience and yourself. For instance, a talk on *Home Decorating* could start with *'How many of you have tried to hang wallpaper to find it has indeed been hung — everywhere except on the wall?'* The nods from your audience show that you have engaged them. If you can intrigue them at the same time, so much the better.

startling statement or question — Make your audience sit up with these, in other words, engage by arrest. A talk on *Population Problems* could begin with *'For every second that I talk to you, three more babies have been born into this world. By the time I have finished, there will be over 10,000 more mouths to feed'.* A talk on *Reincarnation* could well begin with *'Do we remember the past? Have we been here before . . .?'*

quotation — This is always a good beginning, and one for which there are abundant sources such as Benham's Book of Quotations or the Oxford Book of Quotations. A well known quotation establishes rapport with your audience.

relevant example – This could be a short anecdote concerned with the subject. It might be a personal experience which has prompted you to choose your topic for the speech.

humorous remark – Unless you are very experienced and have excellent timing and assurance, this approach step should be avoided. However, if you are confident enough, a laugh from the audience would certainly break the ice at the start of the address.

2 In stating your general aim you tell the audience in broad terms what your subject is. By so doing you indicate to the audience its wider connections and proceed with further specification.

3 Clarification of your aim is, in fact, a limitation of the previous step. A wide subject has been stated, so that its narrow aspect could be indicated here. For example *'Tonight, I'd like to introduce you to the world of advertising, and in particular, to tell you about the methods of ensuring coverage of a product in your home'.*

4 Preview is an optional step, and may appear to be unsubtle. Nevertheless, it can be used effectively to inform the audience of the main points to be covered in the talk.

99 THE DEVELOPMENT. The purposes here are to enlighten, to encompass and to enthuse your audience. You enlighten by presenting the facts, you encompass by involving the audience and you enthuse by your personality and infectious interest in your subject. There are several methods of developing the talk and of course they overlap.

(a) **Chronological development.** Suitable titles here would be *"The life of Mozart", "The history of explosives", "The life cycle of the may fly"*. Time sequence talks are possibly the easiest to construct. One must be sure that the main points are logically arranged and that there are no time gaps.

(b) **Spatial development.** This is the geographical arrangement of the subject material – east to west, inside to outside. Typical subjects here could be *"Planning your garden", "The Island of Cyprus"*, etc.

(c) **Parts of a whole.** This needs careful planning and note headings should be used so that no part is omitted. The subject is chosen and beneath it all the aspects concerned with it are collected. For instance a talk on *"Perception"* could be sub-divided into the use of the eyes, ears, nose, taste buds, tactile elements and extra sensory powers.

(d) **Development by qualities.** This is similar to development by parts of a whole. An object, organisation or a living organism is chosen and all the qualities attributed to it discussed in turn. For instance a talk on *"Boxer Dogs"* could include the ideal features considered by show judges, such as length of tail, features of the head, the shape of the snout, alignment of the legs, and so on.

(e) **Cause and effect.** Here a situation is described and the events leading to its features traced. On the other hand a dramatic event may be postulated and its resulting consequences discussed. The possibilities here are numerous, examples are *"The result of chemical spraying of crops"*, *"Atomic tests and our future"*, *"The drug problem"*.

(f) **Development by definition.** This method of organisation would be appropriate for scientific subjects, where each aspect of a topic is described and defined. For example a talk on *"Atomic energy"* could be developed by defining all the particles in the atom and describing their features and functions.

(g) **Comparison and contrast.** Certain subjects lend themselves to a summary of likenesses and differences. A talk on *"Modern trends in language training"* could contain the methods used in this country and compare or contrast them with those used in America or on the Continent.

You can add to this list considering other means of development such as 'problem and solution', 'structure and function' and so on.

100 THE CONCLUSION. This final step should leave the audience in a state of satisfaction. Try to enlist your audience so that they will consider what you have said, after the talk. There are, again, four simple ways to conclude your speech:

a **a reiteration** — Give a brief summary of the main points made in the talk, but do not make the whole speech again.

b **a startling statement or question** — This is self-explanatory.
   However, in an informative talk, try not to leave an air of gloom
   and despondency. End on a positive note.

c **an anecdote** — a simple relevant story for the audience to
   consider.

d **a humorous remark** — By this time you will know how you can
   handle the audience, and whether you can safely handle a
   light-hearted ending, where you send the listeners away with a
   smile. If you can do this, it always creates a good atmosphere.

THE PERSUASIVE TALK

101 This is speech designed to get others want, believe or do
what you want them to, by appealing to their reason and their
emotions.

Appealing to Reason

Largely depends upon presenting logical proofs such as examples,
analogies, statistics and testimony. Let us examine each of these in
turn:

examples — start with a proposition and support it with factual
descriptions; or cite examples and draw a conclusion
from them. For instance, you could present a list of
factors to be improved, and then state how it could
be be accomplished, eg. a certain establishment has to
deal with a known amount of crockery and cutlery —
you can present a clear account of all the work
involved in washing and cleaning the items, and then
put forward your more efficient plan involving a
special machine and washing powder.

analogies — draw similarities between problems and point out
how one has been solved. It follows, then, that by
adopting the same principles, the other problem
should be solved as well.

statistics — it has been said that 'figures can't lie, but liars can
figure'. However, the presentation of facts and figures

is impressive, and can be a great aid to developing a persuasive speech. Make sure that your figures are accurate, and know the sources and reliability of them. Avoid loose references such as 'figures have proved . . .' etc. You can be challenged by 'What figures, where do you get them?'

testimony — can either be an expert opinion or a common opinion. An expert opinion is one given by an authority in a particular field, eg. by a dentist proposing the use of a certain toothpaste. Common opinion can be given by the man in the street, eg. and ordinary workman's opinion of a brand of beer will be appreciated by other ordinary workmen. The opinion of a well-known personality is also often widely accepted, even if the personality is not an expert in the field under consideration.

Appealing to Emotion

102 Here, one should aim to appeal to man's basic drives and emotional needs. A little consideration and reference to the hoards of adverts around us, will soon convince you of the power of this type of appeal. Basically, there are four aspects of such appeal:

1   **to a person's security** — concerning himself, his family, friends, country, home, job, savings, future, old age, freedom, beliefs, rights, independence etc. One could hardly exhaust all the aspects of life which can provide us with a sense of security.

2   **to a person's sense of adventure** — the need for new experiences in home life, professional and social life — the need for opportunities to invent, create, build, organise, participate in, compete with, appreciate and enjoy.

3   **to the need for recognition** — one wants to be recognised and accorded status by one's family, friends, neighbours and employers — one wants to be respected for one's acquisitions, authority, efficiency, professional contributions and community service.

4   **to the need for response** — one wants to be loved, wanted, needed and understood by one's family, friends, neighbours and employers.

Persuasive 'Crafts'

Take care over your appearance — your looks, dress, manners and bearing. Be warm, friendly and human. Show respect for your listener, don't belittle him. Manifest honesty and fairness to opponents and never get into an argument unnecessarily. Persuade though appeal to emotions such as your listener's fear, anger, love, joy, hate, loyalty, pride, reverence, grief, awe, curiosity, sympathy, respect, etc. Be positive in your presentation of facts and choice of words. Use symbols such as flags or banners — people like to be identified with a movement symbolised by a badge. Avoid crystalising contrary ideas — stick to your points and concentrate the audience's attention on them. Thus, attention can persist long after the talk has ended.